Starters
as a main meal

Starters
as a main meal

Mary-Lou Arnold   Jane Aspinwall   Douglas Marsland
Duske Teape-Davis   Jan Wunderlich

BAY BOOKS
SYDNEY AND LONDON

Photography: Tom Hennemann
Front cover photograph: Ashley Barber
Cookery Editor: Elizabeth Carden
Recipe testing: Karen Davidson, Pat Fenton

Published by Bay Books Pty Ltd
61–69 Anzac Parade,
KENSINGTON NSW 2033

© Bay Books

Publisher: George Barber
National Library of Australia
Card Number and ISBN 1 86256 011 0

Contents

The publisher wishes to thank the following for their generous assistance during the photography of this book:
Peters of Kensington, Anzac Parade, Kensington, NSW; Hale Importers for Pilliuvuyt, 43 Orchard Road, Brookvale, NSW; Sunbeam Corporation, Wade Street, Campsie, NSW; Dansab Imports, 79 Myrtle Street, Chippendale, NSW.

BB86

Introduction

With eating out and home entertaining now so much a part of everyday business and social life, eating patterns have changed — of necessity. Today, one finds only the most dedicated gourmand indulging, on a regular basis, in the three or more rich and flamboyant courses, so long considered traditional fare.

Instead, it has become determinedly chic to eschew such heavy-duty meals in favour of several light and simple, but exquisitely imaginative, offerings. This is where a menu with a dazzling array of first courses is set to flourish.

Call it what you will — entree, starter, appetiser, primo or even vorgang — the first course has come into its own. Diners are increasingly opting for a meal of two starters, rather than one leading up to the main event. In this light, every first course should be able to stand alone and appetise, rather than simply appease until the main meal arrives.

PRESENTATION

What these introductory courses lack in quantity they counterbalance in visual appeal — every dish must be a feast to the eyes as well as the palate.

Exquisite china, glassware and cutlery together with flowers to complement the food will create a magnificent background to a meal. Each dish should itself be contrived with care for visual detail. This means an awareness of colour and shape, with an eye for clever arrangement of the food together with attractive garnishes.

While there's nothing so uninspiring as a drab dish of blandly hued ingredients, a first course that's over-decorated can be equally off-putting.

It is easy to be overawed by the elaborate creations of famous chefs but, in fact, many visually effective flourishes to a dish are quite effortlessly achieved. A sense of style and a simple approach is often the answer.

The Japanese are masters of the art with their subtle contrasts of colour and clever juxtapositioning of food for garnishes. For example, they will create an eye-catching picture in the uncluttered presentation of sashimi — a plate of raw fish. The slices of fish, in contrasting colours, are fanned out across a lacquered board, relieved only by a bundle of grated radish, a dash of greenery and carrot carved into a flower shape bearing a knob of bright green horseradish. The arrangement takes seconds, the impact lasts.

Yakitori

Pumpkin Marsala Soup

A DELICATE BALANCE

With a meal of 'first' courses, balance and complement the dishes. If one dish is light the next can be a little more elaborate or strongly flavoured. This selection of carefully chosen starters will let you create a beautifully balanced meal of two or three courses whether you plan an elaborate evening's entertaining or a simple supper.

Besides refining the palate, a dedication to beautifully contrived but sparing portions also alters expectations. Living as we do in a culture geared to over-indulgence, replacing an over-full stomach with the pleasure of perceptively prepared and elegantly presented dishes is a step towards healthier living standards.

The recipes we have selected take into account the principles of 'nouvelle cuisine' with its emphasis on food that is lightly cooked and served to preserve flavour, texture and nutrients. We hope these recipes and photographs will fire your imagination, stimulate the appetite and satisfy the discerning palate.

QUALITY NOT QUANTITY

With first courses, small is beautiful. The advantage of these 'bonnes bouches' is that they possess an allure which might well evaporate, should the dish be served on a grander scale. A portion of foie gras, a fricassee of kidneys and sweetbreads or a platter of escargots are tempting as starters yet they may be over-powering as a main course. Also, the nicest things do come in small parcels, and dishes which have no pretensions beyond providing a tasty morsel can often encapsulate the best in a culture or style of cuisine — for instance, Italian gnocchi, Arabian meat loaf or a simple potage.

When serving only a small portion, it is doubly important that what one is offering should be an exquisite appetiser composed with the finest ingredients. Whether this is an economical pasta dish or an extravagant creation with caviar, the impact will be greatest where care and concern are shown in seeking out quality produce. This often requires resolve in insisting on only the best cuts of meat, fish or cheese, picking over fruit and salad ingredients for young, fresh, tender and unbruised leaves and hunting down fresh herbs instead of settling for the dried ones.

A little dedication and perseverance in pursuing just the right ingredients will elevate a first course from the pedestrian to the sublime. This can be achieved simply by taking the trouble to find, for example, wild mushrooms, or just a few grams of fresh truffles or by investing in walnut or hazelnut oil instead of the more regular olive oil.

Today there are very few foods that may truly be considered seasonal; modern transport systems make it possible to convey even the most fragile produce from one hemisphere to the other in a matter of days or even hours.

However, there is little sense in complicating a menu by selecting dishes with ingredients that are all but impossible to locate. Limited availability also restricts the range of quality so, as a rule, it is better to make use of produce that's in reasonably plentiful supply.

Smoked Salmon Quiche

Broccoli Terrine

Blini

TO SUBSTITUTE . . . OR NOT?

There are occasions when one might be forgiven for making substitutions in a recipe, particularly where the impact is visual. For instance, turmeric is a useful and low cost alternative to saffron as a colouring agent — but is no substitute for saffron's more subtle flavour. The same applies to caviar; while there is no rival to Beluga or Sevruga, the very economically priced lumpfish roe is an excellent substitute for garnishing.

But stray too far from ingredients specified in a recipe and one runs the risk of losing the concept of 'fine cuisine'. The beauty of a first course is that its paucity lets you aim for the very best; parsimony with costly, exotic or innovative ingredients will very likely leave the final product wanting while the addition of thickening agents, uninvited cream, butter or seasonings will gild the lily quite unnecessarily.

Never be afraid to innovate and experiment. Bear in mind, however, that each dish should stand by its own virtues and not overwhelm whatever is to follow.

EQUIPMENT: THE ESSENTIALS

With cooking, as with every other skill, it is essential to work with the proper equipment. For the best results, whether for family meals or for entertaining, saucepans, casseroles, quiche dishes and kitchen utensils etc. should be good quality ones. Choosing equipment that will last a long time will repay any initial investment.

ELECTRICAL EQUIPMENT

In most kitchens today, the electric blender and food processor are standard items. The processor, which purees, chops, shreds, slices and grates, is a great labour saver. But people did prepare wonderful meals without it, once upon a time. Many recipes in this book call for ingredients to be shredded or pureed. For those who do not have a food processor or blender, don't forget the old-fashioned grater, the sieve plus wooden spoon and the foodmill. They do a great job and are easy to clean up afterwards.

MEASURING EQUIPMENT

Most ingredients in this book are given in cups and spoons — a very simple and reliable method for measuring quantities. A set of metric cups and spoons and a liquid measuring jug are essential kitchen utensils. You will need a nest of cups for measuring dry ingredients (1 cup, ½ cup, ⅓ cup and ¼ cup); a set of spoons (1 tablespoon, 1 teaspoon, ½ teaspoon and ¼ teaspoon); and a transparent graduated measuring jug (1 litre or 250 mL) for measuring liquids. Cup and spoon measures are always level. Simply spoon in the dry ingredients and level off with the back of a knife. The standard metric measures are:

1 cup	250 mL
1 tablespoon	20 mL
1 teaspoon	5 mL

Quantities for butter, some prepackaged items and fresh ingredients such as vegetables and meat are given in grams. For accuracy it is important to use scales to weigh these ingredients.

Soups

Too often, the arrival of soup is greeted with ill-concealed disappointment. It is seen as being ballast to appease the appetites of guests who are eagerly awaiting the main course, the *pièce de résistance*. In a meal where all courses are equal, soup plays a vital role in complementing the complete menu.

A slightly piquant Gazpacho (*see recipe*) makes a cool entry to a summer luncheon, while an impressive Prawn Chowder (*see recipe*) is comparatively rich and filling. Curried Chicken Soup (*see recipe*) juxtaposes hot and cold, while clever combinations of flavour, like carrot and orange, inject an element of surprise and delight into a dinner party.

Don't let soups look dull. Just a dash of a contrasting garnish — a swirl of cream or a scattering of croutons or a sprinkle of freshly chopped herbs — and that bowl of soup becomes a visual delight.

COLD SOUPS

CURRIED CHICKEN SOUP

The hot and cold contrast creates the element of surprise in this unusual summer soup that can also be served hot in cooler weather.

30 g butter or ghee
1 large onion, diced
2 celery stalks with green
   tops, sliced
1 tablespoon curry
   powder
3 tablespoons flour
2 large green apples,
   roughly chopped
250 g cooked chicken
   meat, chopped
1.25 litres chicken stock
1 tablespoon lemon juice
salt and pepper, to taste
natural yoghurt or
   thickened cream
chopped chives

Melt butter in a large pan and cook onion and celery for about 5 minutes until softened. Add curry powder and flour and cook for 3 minutes, stirring occasionally to prevent sticking. Add apple, chicken and 1 cup of stock and simmer for about 5 minutes. Cool slightly.

Puree mixture in a food processor or blender. This may need to be done in several batches. Return puree to pan and add the remaining chicken stock, the lemon juice, salt and pepper. Bring to boil and simmer for about 10 minutes to bring out the flavour.

Cool soup then cover and chill in refrigerator. Serve cold with a spoonful of yoghurt or cream in each bowl and a sprinkle of chopped chives.

Serves 4

Left to right: Curried Chicken Soup, Prawn Chowder (see recipes)

Chilled Avocado Soup

CHILLED AVOCADO SOUP

2 large ripe avocados
2 shallots, chopped
  roughly
3 cups chicken stock
300 mL thickened cream
  (double cream)

salt to taste
ground pepper
chopped dill

Peel 1 avocado and roughly chop and puree it in a food processor. Add shallots and puree until smooth. Slowly blend in the chicken stock.

Transfer the soup to a bowl, add the cream and season to taste. To chill the soup, place the avocado seed back in the bowl as this will prevent discolouring. Cover with clear plastic wrap and chill thoroughly.

Just before serving, cut the second avocado in half, remove seed and scoop out flesh with melon baller. Sprinkle avocado balls with lemon juice to prevent discolouring.

Serve soup cold (remembering to remove the seed) garnished with the avocado balls and chopped dill.

Serves 4

GAZPACHO

Gazpacho is a chilled Spanish soup served with ice cubes and with the garnishes presented in individual bowls so that everyone can help themselves.

½ cup fresh
    breadcrumbs
½ cup ground almonds
3 cloves garlic, crushed
2 tablespoons olive oil
1 teaspoon paprika
1 teaspoon salt
1 teaspoon sugar
cayenne pepper, to taste
1 tablespoon vinegar
8 large ripe tomatoes,
    peeled and seeded

1 red capsicum (pepper),
    seeded and chopped
1 cucumber, peeled,
    seeded and chopped
1 Spanish onion, peeled
    and chopped (brown or
    white onions can be
    substituted)
1½ cups clear chicken
    stock
1½ cups tomato juice

GARNISH

1 cup croutons, cooked in
    garlic-flavoured olive
    oil
1 green capsicum
    (pepper), diced

1 cucumber, diced
1 onion, diced
ice cubes

Combine the breadcrumbs, ground almonds, crushed garlic, olive oil, paprika, salt, sugar, cayenne pepper and vinegar and set aside.

Blend tomatoes, capsicum (peppers), cucumber and onion in food processor. Add spices to puree and blend until thoroughly mixed. Transfer soup to a large bowl; and add chicken stock and tomato juice. Chill covered with plastic wrap.

Prepare garnishes and arrange each in a separate bowl. Serve the soup with the ice cubes and bowls of garnishes.

Serves 6

VICHYSSOISE

1 white onion
4 leeks, well washed
60 g butter
1 litre chicken stock
1 tablespoon chopped
    parsley

1 stalk celery, chopped
3 potatoes, peeled and
    sliced thinly
salt and pepper
1¼ cups milk
1¼ cups cream

GARNISH

1 cup whipped cream

leek needles

Slice the onion and the white part of the leek finely. Melt butter in saucepan and cook leek and onion gently until tender. Do not let them brown. Add chicken stock, chopped parsley, celery, potatoes, salt and pepper and simmer for 15 minutes. Cool slightly, puree then strain through a sieve.

Test for flavour and adjust seasonings if desired. Add milk and cream and reheat. Cool and chill thoroughly.

Serve Vichyssoise in chilled bowls. Float a little whipped cream on the soup and top with curly leek needles.

Serves 6

LEEK NEEDLES: GETTING THEM TO CURL

Prepare leek needles from the soft green tops of the leek. Shred these finely and drop them into iced water so they will curl. Drain and use as a garnish with Vichyssoise.

Vichyssoise

HOT SOUPS

HOT SPICED TOMATO SOUP

This is a quick and effortless soup that can be spiced with 2 tablespoons of vodka for special occasions.

1.25 litres fresh or
  canned tomato juice
1 cup canned vegetable
  juice (such as V8)
4 beef stock cubes
2 teaspoons lemon juice
dash Tabasco

freshly ground black
  pepper
6 sprigs of mint or thin
  slices of lemon, to
  garnish

Combine tomato and vegetable juices and heat through (preferably in an enamel or stainless steel pan). Do not boil. Crush beef stock cubes, dissolve in ½ cup of the hot juice and return to pan. Bring to boil and flavour with lemon juice, Tabasco and pepper. Serve garnished with a sprig of mint or a thin slice of lemon.

Serves 6

AVGOLEMONO

1.25 litres rich chicken
  stock
⅓ cup long grain rice
2 eggs

juice 1 lemon
salt and pepper
6 lemon slices

Bring chicken stock to the boil, stir in rice and simmer about 15–20 minutes until rice is tender.

Beat eggs and lemon juice together in a bowl until well blended.

Gradually stir in a little (about 2 tablespoons) of the boiling soup to the egg and lemon mixture. Now add 2 cups soup and stir until it is slightly thickened. Whisk combined mixture back into remaining soup and heat through. **Do not boil** or the soup will curdle.

Season to taste and serve hot with lemon slices.

Serves 6

PRAWN CHOWDER

2 bacon rashers, diced
60 g butter
1 cup finely chopped
  onion
2 cups peeled and diced
  potato
salt and pepper

1 cup chicken stock
500 g peeled, cooked
  prawns or cubes of
  sauteed fish
2 cups milk
½ cup cream
dash Tabasco

Saute diced bacon until soft in saucepan. Add butter and onion and cook for 5 minutes until onion is golden. Add potato, salt, pepper and chicken stock and cook, covered, until potato is tender. Stir in the prawns, milk and cream, season to taste and heat, **but do not boil.**

Serve with crusty bread.

Serves 4–6

CARROT AND ORANGE SOUP

This versatile soup can be served hot or cold. Prepare ahead of time and reheat or serve chilled as required.

2 teaspoons oil
400 g carrots, chopped
1 large onion, chopped
juice of 2 oranges
2 teaspoons grated
  orange zest

1 litre chicken stock
1 teaspoon curry powder
1 clove garlic, crushed
freshly ground black
  pepper

GARNISH

6 thin slices of orange
6 sprigs of mint

½ cup non-fat natural
  yoghurt

Heat oil in a saucepan, add carrots and onion, and sweat gently for 10 minutes. Add juice, zest, stock, curry powder, garlic and pepper. Simmer until carrots are tender. Cool slightly then puree in a food processor or blender.

To serve hot, reheat and serve in individual bowls with a spoonful of yoghurt and garnished with a thin slice of orange and a sprig of mint.

Serve cold, well chilled and similarly garnished.

Serves 6

Prawn Chowder

Cock-a-leekie

CREAM OF CARROT SOUP

60 g butter
500 g young carrots,
  sliced
1 onion, sliced
2 sticks celery, chopped
2 crushed cardamom pods

1 litre chicken stock
½ cup cream
salt and pepper
½ teaspoon nutmeg
6 slices bread, for bread
  rounds

Melt butter in saucepan, add carrots, onion, celery and cardamom. Cover and sweat gently for 10 minutes, without browning. Add half the stock and bring to the boil. Cover and simmer for 15 minutes until tender. Cool slightly and then puree until well blended and smooth.

Return to saucepan, add remaining stock and cream and heat soup thoroughly without boiling. Season to taste with salt, pepper and nutmeg.

To prepare the bread rounds, lightly toast bread then cut with a fluted pastry or biscuit cutter. Each slice should make 2 bread rounds.

Serves 6

ZUCCHINI SOUP

500 g zucchini
  (courgettes), grated
½ teaspoon sugar
1½ cups water
2 stock cubes
20 g butter

1 tablespoon flour
3 cups milk
2 tablespoons pimiento
  strips or diced red
  capsicum (pepper)
½ cup cream

Cook zucchini in sugared water until tender. Cool slightly, then puree.

Dissolve stock cubes in a little puree and set aside.

Melt butter in a saucepan, stir in flour and gradually add the milk and stock cubes, stirring continually. Cook until thickened slightly. Add zucchini puree and stir in pimiento strips or red capsicum. Cream may be added if desired or served swirled on top of the soup.

Serves 4–6

COCK-A-LEEKIE

2.5 kg chicken
1 litre chicken stock
bouquet garni
90 g pearl barley
10 leeks, trimmed and
  washed
10 prunes, pitted and
  soaked

2 tablespoons chopped
  parsley
2½ teaspoons salt
freshly ground black
  pepper
½ cup cream, optional

Simmer chicken in large, partially covered saucepan with stock, bouquet garni and barley for 40 minutes.

Slice and rinse leeks thoroughly and add them, with the prunes, and cook for a further 15 minutes.

Discard the bouquet garni, and lift out the chicken. Skin and bone chicken and cut the meat into bite-sized pieces, returning these to the pan.

Chill soup then skim fat from the surface. Reheat, adding parsley, salt and pepper to taste. Stir in cream if you wish, simmer and serve.

Serves 6

Minestrone

MINESTRONE

2 tablespoons olive oil
2 cloves garlic, crushed
1 large onion, diced
1 stalk celery, diced
3 carrots, sliced
3 zucchini (courgettes),
  sliced
1 cup peas, shelled (or
  frozen peas)
¼ small cabbage,
  shredded
1 teaspoon fresh
  rosemary
4 bacon rashers, diced

450 g fresh tomatoes,
  skinned, seeded and
  chopped or 425 g can
  peeled tomatoes
2 litres beef stock
bay leaf, parsley sprigs
  (tied in muslin)
220 g can borlotti beans
100 g macaroni
salt and pepper to taste
5 tablespoons grated
  Romano cheese, to
  serve
hot garlic or herbed
  bread, to serve

Heat olive oil in large pan and saute garlic and onion until golden. Then lightly cook remaining vegetables (not frozen peas if used) for 10 minutes, stirring occasionally. Sprinkle in rosemary, remove vegetables from pan and set aside.

Fry diced bacon until crisp and brown then drain and also set aside.

Place the vegetables, tomatoes, beef stock and herb bag in a large saucepan, bring to the boil and simmer for 20 minutes, partially covered. Add cooked bacon, beans (frozen peas if used) and macaroni, and simmer a further 15–20 minutes.

Discard the herb bag, adjust seasoning, sprinkle with grated Romano cheese and serve.

Serves 8–10

BORSCHT

A popular soup served in both Poland and Russia accompanied with pirozhki or rye bread.

2 tablespoons oil
2 onions, thinly sliced
500 g shin beef, trimmed
    and cut into cubes
1.75 litres beef stock
salt and pepper
sprigs thyme, bay leaf
    and chopped garlic
    clove tied together in
    muslin
2 carrots, chopped

1 white turnip, chopped
½ small cabbage,
    shredded
4 tomatoes, peeled,
    seeded and chopped
1 bunch beetroot, peeled
    and grated
1¼ cups sour (dairy
    soured) cream, lightly
    beaten

Heat oil in large saucepan, add onions, then meat and saute until golden brown. Pour in stock and season with salt, pepper and herbs. Bring to the boil, add the vegetables, cover the pan and simmer gently for 1 hour. Then add tomatoes and simmer for another 30 minutes.

At this point the soup may be stored in the refrigerator to save time later on. In the final stages, reheat the soup and add the peeled and grated beetroot to the warmed mixture 15 minutes before serving. Do not boil from now on as beetroot discolours.

Serve topped with a swirl of sour cream in each bowl.

Serves 8

CROUTONS

Delicious as a garnish for soup.

½ loaf day old bread
oil for frying

Remove the crust and cut the bread into 1 cm cubes. Heat the oil for deep-frying in a straight-sided pan. Add the bread cubes a few at a time and fry until they are golden brown. Drain on paper towel. Repeat with remaining cubes of bread.

PUMPKIN MARSALA SOUP

3 bacon rashers, diced
40 g butter
1 kg pumpkin (butternut)
    peeled, seeded and
    diced
1 litre beef stock
3 tablespoons dry
    Marsala
1 teaspoon dried thyme

pinch nutmeg or cumin
salt and freshly ground
    black pepper
½ cup cream
toasted pumpkin seeds,
    to garnish
dusting of paprika, to
    garnish

Cook bacon until crisp. Remove from pan and set aside, reserving the fat. Add butter and melt. Add pumpkin and gently sweat until light golden. Add stock and simmer for about 15 minutes or until tender. Cool slightly then add Marsala, herbs and spice to taste.

Puree soup until smooth then return to pan and add bacon. Simmer for 10 minutes until heated through.

Add ½ cup cream if desired or serve cream separately so people can add their own.

Garnish with pumpkin seeds, dust with paprika and serve soup in a tureen or in individual bowls.

Serves 6

CALLALOO

500 g Chinese spinach
    and cabbage, mixed
1 litre chicken stock
1 medium onion, finely
    chopped
1 clove garlic, crushed
2 sprigs thyme
3 bacon rashers, chopped

250 g can crabmeat
250 g can okra, drained
    (or fresh in season)
Tabasco
salt and freshly ground
    black pepper

Wash and coarsely chop spinach and cabbage, simmering them in a large pot with chicken stock, onion, garlic, thyme and bacon. When ingredients are tender add crabmeat and okra and simmer for a further 10 minutes. Season to taste by adding Tabasco, salt and pepper.

Serves 6

Pasta

The beauty of pasta is the ease with which it can be transformed into a stunning dish. The fresh varieties are preferable to dried and nowadays these are more readily available. Both fresh and dried pasta should be added to rapidly boiling water. The fresh pasta takes about 3–5 minutes to cook whilst the dried pasta takes longer — approximately 12 minutes. Pasta should be served 'al dente' meaning literally 'to the tooth' and not overcooked.

Pasta has long been saddled with a reputation as kilojoule-laden and starchy. In fact, it is now highly recommended by nutrition pundits for its food value. Being bulky food, it is particularly well-suited to entree-sized portions. Its subtle flavour provides an excellent accompaniment to distinctively flavoured herbs, cheeses, meats and fish.

Pasta's different shapes and colours make it an eye-catching treat if served with just a little garlic butter and freshly ground black pepper. A medley of natural coloured, green and red fettuccine looks just as inviting as it tastes.

Pasta can be served in numerous forms — fettuccine, spaghetti, lasagne, ravioli, tortellini and gnocchi are all tantalising variations on the theme. The delicious recipes in this chapter will provide enthusiastic cooks with opportunities to experiment to develop their own ideas and tastes with an individual flair.

PENNE WITH PARSLEY AND WATERCRESS

1/3 cup olive oil
1/3 cup chopped parsley
1/3 cup chopped watercress
2 tablespoons chopped capers
1 clove garlic, crushed
salt, to taste
freshly ground black pepper
1/4 cup lemon juice
250 g penne noodles
40 g unsalted butter
12 cherry tomatoes
watercress sprigs

Gradually adding the olive oil, puree parsley, watercress, capers, garlic, salt and pepper together. Pour in lemon juice and blend thoroughly.

Cook the penne in boiling water for 4 minutes if fresh, 12 minutes if dried. Drain and toss penne with unsalted butter.

Pour the green sauce over individual portions, garnish with cherry tomatoes and watercress sprigs and serve.

Serves 4–6

Artichoke and Sausage Fettuccine

ARTICHOKE AND SAUSAGE FETTUCCINE

125 g Danish salami
1 onion, chopped
2 cloves garlic, crushed
½ cup dry white wine
1 cup chicken stock
220 g canned artichoke
  hearts, drained and
  quartered

250 g fettuccine
60 g unsalted butter
salt and pepper
⅓ cup Parmesan cheese
2 tablespoons finely
  chopped parsley
½ red capsicum (pepper)
  cut into strips

Remove skin casing from salami, chop the meat up roughly and combine with onion and garlic in a pan. Fry gently until the onion is golden, then add wine and stock. Bring to the boil then simmer, covered, for 15 minutes. Add artichoke hearts and cook for a further 5 minutes, then set aside the covered pan.

Cook fettuccine in boiling salted water for 8 minutes, then drain and toss with unsalted butter. Combine fettuccine with the artichoke mixture, adding salt and pepper to taste.

Serve in individual portions sprinkled with Parmesan cheese and parsley and garnished with capsicum strips.

Serves 6

TOMATO FETTUCCINE WITH CAULIFLOWER AND OLIVES

½ medium-sized
  cauliflower
4 tomatoes, peeled
½ cup olive oil
1 clove garlic, crushed
30 stuffed olives

250 g red fettuccine
  noodles
60 g ham, diced
½ cup Parmesan cheese
  or pecorino cheese

Break cauliflower into florets and cook in boiling, salted water for 8 minutes, then drain.

Simmer tomatoes, olive oil and garlic over medium heat for 10 minutes, add olives and set aside.

Boil fettuccine in salted water for 8 minutes or until cooked, drain and divide between individual plates.

Combine tomato mixture, cauliflower and ham to complete the sauce which can then be spooned over the fettuccine. Sprinkle with Parmesan cheese and serve hot.

WHOLEMEAL SPAGHETTI WITH CALAMARI

250 g wholemeal
  spaghetti
125 g calamari (squid),
  cleaned
1 tablespoon chopped
  parsley
1 clove garlic, crushed

4 tablespoons olive oil
salt and pepper
1 onion, sliced
3 tablespoons tomato
  paste
extra chopped parsley, to
  garnish

Cook spaghetti in boiling salted water for 10–15 minutes or until cooked, then drain and set aside.

Slice calamari into 3 mm wide rings and combine with parsley, garlic, olive oil, salt, pepper, onion slices and tomato paste in a frying pan. Simmer sauce for 10 minutes.

Serve spaghetti with sauce spooned over the top

Tomato Fettuccine with Cauliflower and Olives

Wash, dry and cut eggplants into 3 mm slices. Combine breadcrumbs and Parmesan cheese and lightly dip eggplant slices first into beaten egg and then into the crumb mix. Fry them in hot oil until golden brown on each side, then drain and set aside.

Leaving 1 tablespoon of oil in the frying pan cook veal, onion, garlic, mushrooms, oregano, tomato paste, salt and pepper for 5 minutes, stirring occasionally. Reduce heat and simmer for 15 minutes.

Meanwhile, boil spaghetti in salted water for 8–10 minutes, remove and drain then combine it with ricotta cheese.

Using large oven-proof dish, place a layer of eggplant on the bottom, cover this with the meat mixture and top it with a layer of spaghetti. Add the sliced hard-boiled eggs, sprinkle with Parmesan cheese and bake in a moderate oven 190°C (375°F) for 20–25 minutes, or until golden brown. Unmould onto a serving plate, cut into wedges, sprinkle with chopped parsley and serve.

Serves 6

CREAMED TORTELLINI VOL-AU-VENT

375 g frozen or fresh tortellini	pinch cinnamon
40 g butter	4 large vol-au-vent cases
¾ cup cream	1 clove garlic, crushed
1 cup Parmesan cheese	freshly ground black pepper
pinch nutmeg	watercress, to garnish

Cook tortellini in boiling water , then drain and set aside.

Mix the butter, cream, ⅔ cup Parmesan cheese, nutmeg, cinnamon, garlic and black pepper to a creamy consistency over a low heat.

Heat vol-au-vent cases in the oven for 5 minutes, then set aside on warm plates until the tortellini is ready.

Combine tortellini and the cream sauce and spoon equal portions into the vol-au-vent cases. Sprinkle remaining Parmesan cheese over each and return the vol-au-vents to the oven for 3 minutes to heat through.

Serve garnished with watercress.

Serves 4

and garnished with the extra chopped parsley.

Serves 4

RICOTTA PASTA CAKE

2 large eggplant (aubergines)	½ teaspoon oregano
1 egg, well beaten	2 tablespoons tomato paste
1 cup breadcrumbs	salt and pepper
1 tablespoon Parmesan cheese, grated	250 g spaghetti
1 cup oil	90 g ricotta cheese
250 g minced veal	3 hard-boiled eggs, shelled
1 onion, finely chopped	⅔ cup Parmesan cheese, grated
2 cloves garlic	chopped parsley
125 g mushrooms, sliced	

PUMPKIN GNOCCHI WITH PARMESAN AND RICOTTA

500 g pumpkin, to make
2 cups mashed
pumpkin
1¼ cups flour
salt to taste

⅔ cup Parmesan cheese
½ cup ricotta cheese
2 tablespoons chopped
parsley

Peel the pumpkin, and boil it in salted water until tender. Drain and mash pumpkin to a smooth puree with flour and salt. Knead the mixture well to achieve a smooth dough. Shape the dough into a log shape and divide it into 2.5 cm pieces.

Cook gnocchi in boiling salted water a few at a time. When they rise to the surface they are ready to be taken out and drained.

Place gnocchi into individual serving dishes and top each portion with Parmesan and ricotta cheeses. Bake at 200°C (400°F) for 10 minutes, or until golden brown. Serve sprinkled with chopped parsley.

Serves 4–6

DEEP-FRIED PASTA BASKET WITH MARINARA SAUCE

250 g egg noodles

3 cups oil for deep-frying

MARINARA SAUCE

500 g raw prawns,
shelled and veins
removed
3 calamari (squid),
cleaned and sliced
250 g scallops
½ cup dry white wine
½ cup water
2 tablespoons oil
5 large tomatoes, peeled
and chopped
2 cloves garlic, crushed

1 tablespoon tomato
paste
8 oysters
45 g can anchovies,
drained
salt
freshly ground black
pepper
1 tablespoon chopped
parsley
Parmesan cheese, to
serve

Cook egg noodles in boiling salted water for 8 minutes, then drain. Using a metal strainer, place ¼ of the noodles into the strainer to form a 'basket' shape. Place a second strainer over the top of the noodles to hold them in place.

Heat the oil and, when it's very hot, lower the strainer into it. Cook noodles until crisp and golden brown, then remove noodle basket from the strainers and allow to drain. Repeat with remaining noodles to make 3 more baskets.

Simmer prawns, calamari, scallops, wine and water in a large saucepan for 1 minute, then remove the seafood and set aside. Heat oil in frying pan, stir in tomatoes, garlic and tomato paste and cook for 2 minutes. Add cooked seafood plus oysters and anchovies to the pan and heat through, seasoning with salt and pepper and adding the parsley.

Place noodle baskets on serving plates and spoon over the Marinara Sauce. Serve hot with a sprinkling of Parmesan cheese.

Serves 4

WHITING LASAGNE ROLLS NEAPOLITAN

2 teaspoons olive oil
12 sheets green lasagne
12 whiting fillets
1 cup water
½ teaspoon dried basil
salt
freshly ground black
pepper
4 tablespoons Parmesan
cheese

4 large tomatoes, peeled
and chopped
1 onion, finely chopped
2 tablespoons chopped
parsley
1 tablespoon oil
1 clove garlic, crushed
½ red capsicum
(pepper), sliced

Cook lasagne sheets 1 at a time in boiling, salted water with 2 teaspoons olive oil. The saucepan should be about ⅔ full. Cook each sheet for 2 minutes — after the water has returned to the boil — then remove lasagne and drain. Continue in this way until all are cooked.

Gently simmer whiting fillets in 1 cup water with basil, salt and pepper for 5 minutes. Remove the fish and place 1 fillet on each sheet of lasagne, sprinkling with Parmesan cheese. Roll up each one and place, seams down, on an ovenproof dish and set aside.

Combine tomatoes, onion, parsley, oil, garlic and capsicum, bringing them to the boil and simmering for 10 minutes. Spoon sauce over the rolls and bake in a hot oven 200°C (400°F) for 15 minutes. Serve 2 rolls per portion with the sauce.

Serves 6

Deep-fried Pasta Basket with Marinara Sauce

Seafood

Delicacy of flavour combined with a refreshing lack of kilojoules makes fish a prized ingredient in thoughtfully composed and innovative cuisine. While it is an excellent foil to piquant marinades and rich sauces, seafood does not overshadow fragile flavourings, such as saffron, which are in danger of eclipse from more strongly flavoured meat dishes.

Its variety in shape, size, texture and colouring provide enormous potential in the presentation of seafood dishes. This is especially important in serving entree-sized portions.

While one may be uninspired by a slab of white fish drenched in a blandly coloured sauce, the same ingredients become enormously alluring when artfully arranged and carefully garnished.

More than perhaps any other food, fish is enlivened by gentle cooking, thoughtful preparation and imaginative presentation; bear these cardinal rules in mind and each creation will be a triumph.

OYSTERS MACQUARIE

360 g cooked lobster tail, cut into 2 cm cubes
36 fresh oysters on the shell
1¼ cups Cocktail Sauce (see recipe)
¼ red capsicum (pepper), finely chopped
1 truffle, diced or caviar
6 lemon wedges, with pips removed
4 slices brown bread, remove crusts, cut into triangles and butter

Place 1 cube of lobster on top of each oyster and brush with Cocktail Sauce. Top with diced capsicum and choppd truffle or caviar.

Serve on individual plates — 6 per plate — with a lemon wedge and bread triangles.

Serves 6

Brochette of Mussels

Oysters Zingara

Remove the mussels and strain the liquid through a fine sieve or cheesecloth to extract any particles of dirt.

Pour the cooking liquid into a clean saucepan, making it up to 250 mL by adding fish stock if necessary. Add butter and bring to the boil.

Serve by arranging the mussels in hot soup plates, pouring sauce over them and adding a sprinkling of chopped parsley. Accompany with hot crusty French bread.

Serves 4–6

BROCHETTE OF MUSSELS

48 mussels, in shells
½ cup white wine
1 tablespoon chopped
   parsley stalks
1 small onion, chopped
¼ teaspoon dried thyme
1 bay leaf
salt
freshly ground pepper

3–4 rindless bacon
   rashers, cut into thirds
1 cup seasoned flour
2 beaten eggs
fine breadcrumbs
cooking oil, for deep-
   frying
Easy Bearnaise Sauce
   (see recipe), for serving

Scrub mussel shells thoroughly and wash them in salted water. Boil them in a covered pan with wine, parsley stalks, onion, thyme, bay leaf, salt and pepper until the shells open; this should take about 4–5 minutes.

Cool, then remove mussels from their shells and thread 6 onto each satay stick with a bacon roll between each one.

Roll each brochette in seasoned flour, dip in beaten egg and roll in fine breadcrumbs, then deep-fry in hot oil until golden. Drain on absorbent paper. Serve 2 sticks per portion, accompanied by Easy Bearnaise Sauce if you wish.

Serves 4

OYSTERS ZINGARA

6 hard-boiled eggs
36 fresh oysters on the
   shell
200 g red caviar
12 small brown rolls,
   buttered

6 lemon wedges, seeded
6 sprigs parsley or
   watercress

Sieve yolks and whites of eggs separately. Cover ⅓ of each oyster with sieved yolk, then top with a scoop of red caviar. Finally spoon enough egg white over the oyster to cover surface. Serve chilled with small buttered rolls and lemon wedges, garnished with sprigs of parsley or watercress.

Serves 6

MUSSELS WITH WHITE WINE

48 mussels, in shells
1 cup dry white wine
3 shallots (spring onions,
   scallions), finely
   chopped
6 parsley stalks, chopped
1 bay leaf

½ teaspoon fresh thyme
1 teaspoon freshly
   ground pepper
60 g butter
chopped parsley

Scrub mussel shells thoroughly then bring to the boil in a large covered saucepan with wine, shallots, parsley, bay leaf, thyme and pepper until the shells all open — it should only take about 4–5 minutes.

Chilled Mussel Salad

CHILLED MUSSEL SALAD

2 kg mussels, in shells
1 cup wine
1 cup water
few sprigs parsley

3 bay leaves
1 teaspoon black
   peppercorns

DRESSING

¼ cup white wine
   vinegar
salt and pepper
1 teaspoon French
   mustard
¾ cup oil
4 eggs, hard-boiled

¼ cup chopped parsley
¾ teaspoon chopped
   fresh tarragon
1 teaspoon snipped
   chives
2 teaspoons chopped
   gherkins

Prepare the mussels for cooking by scrubbing them well and discarding any with open shells. With a vegetable knife, remove the 'beard'.

Bring the wine, water, parsley, bay leaves and peppercorns to the boil in a large pan then lower heat and simmer for 5 minutes. Add the mussels, cover and simmer until they open, about 3–5 minutes. Now remove the mussels from their shells, pouring off any cooking liquid or pieces of flavouring. Arrange the mussels in individual serving dishes discarding any that do not open.

Whisk vinegar, salt, pepper and mustard well to combine. Gradually add the oil, whisking constantly. Taste and adjust the seasoning.

Chop the hard-boiled eggs and add to the dressing with the parsley, tarragon, chives and gherkins, stirring to combine. Leave for 30 minutes for the flavours to blend and develop. Stir again then pour evenly over the mussels.

Toss lightly so that all the mussels are coated with the dressing then chill until serving time.

Chilled Mussel Salad is delicious served with crusty bread and lemon wedges.

Serves 4–6

Shellfish Cocktail

PRAWNS PROVENCALE

500 g uncooked prawns
2½ tablespoons cooking
  oil
1 small clove garlic
250 g ripe tomatoes,
  peeled, seeded and
  chopped
2 tablespoons dry white
  wine

½ cup Fresh Tomato
  Sauce (see recipe)
coarsely chopped parsley
lime or lemon slices and
  parsley sprigs, to
  garnish

Lightly coat prawns with seasoned flour and shake off the surplus. Heat 2 tablespoons of the oil in frying pan and add the prawns, frying to a light golden brown colour and tossing frequently. Drain prawns well.

Fry garlic in remaining oil in a saucepan for a few seconds, pour off any surplus oil then add the tomatoes, cooking them 8–10 minutes.

Add white wine and Fresh Tomato Sauce and bring to the boil. Adjust seasonings to taste and stir in the chopped parsley. Now gently fold the prawns through the sauce.

Serve on individual plates, garnished with lime or lemon slices and sprig of parsley.

Serves 4

SEAFOOD VOL-AU-VENT

4 vol-au-vent cases, pre-
  cooked
250 g cooked seafood
  (lobster, prawns,
  mussels, scallops)
60 g button mushrooms

30 g butter
1 tablespoon lemon juice
½ cup White Wine
  Sauce (see recipe)
chopped parsley
salt and pepper

Warm vol-au-vent cases while preparing the seafood mixture. Peel and wash mushrooms, cut into dice and cook in butter and lemon juice for 2–3 minutes. Add the prepared seafood, the White Wine Sauce, parsley and seasonings.

Spoon seafood mixture into warm vol-au-vent cases and serve on individual plates.

Serves 4

PAN-FRIED BUTTERFLY PRAWNS

12 large uncooked
  prawns
3 long bacon rashers
¼ teaspoon pepper
1¼ tablespoons oil
¼ cup tomato sauce

¼ cup hoi sin sauce
  (Chinese barbecue
  sauce)
6 lime wedges

Shell prawns, leaving tail intact, remove veins and cut in half lengthways from head to tail. Remove rind from bacon and cut each rasher into 4 pieces. Wrap 1 piece of bacon around the tail of each prawn and fasten with a toothpick. Fold each strip of prawn meat back and fasten onto toothpick. Sprinkle with pepper.

Heat oil and fry prawns on each side until pink. Stir in tomato and hoi sin sauces and cook until hot. Allow 2–3 prawns per serve. Garnish with wedges of lime.

Serves 4–6

COQUILLES ST JACQUES

24 shelled scallops
1 egg beaten with a little
   milk
1 cup Mornay Sauce (see
   recipe)

½ cup Parmesan cheese
lemon wedges and
   parsley sprigs, to
   garnish

DUCHESS POTATO

500 g potatoes, peeled
   and cooked
1 egg yolk

1½ tablespoons butter or
   margarine
salt and pepper, to taste

First prepare Duchess Potato by mashing potatoes well so there are no lumps and stirring in the egg yolk and butter and seasonings so that you have a piping consistency.

Bring scallops slowly to boil, skim, lower heat and simmer until cooked (about 5 minutes). Slice and set aside.

Pipe a border of Duchess Potato around 4 scallop shells using a large star tube. Brush with a little beaten egg and milk combined and dry in moderate oven 180°C (350°F) or under the grill for 2–3 minutes.

Warm Mornay Sauce and pour a little into the bottom of each shell, arrange the scallop slices and coat with remaining sauce taking care not to splash the potato piping. Sprinkle with Parmesan cheese and brown under the grill.

Serve garnished with lemon wedges and a sprig of parsley.

Serves 4

SHELLFISH COCKTAIL

200 g prepared crab,
   lobster, prawns
¼ lettuce
½ cup Cocktail Sauce
   (see recipe)
4 teaspoons red or black
   caviar

4 lemon wedges, pips
   removed
4 parsley sprigs
triangles of buttered
   bread

To prepare seafood, shred the white meat of the crab; chop lobster into 1.5 cm dice; peel, remove intestinal track and wash prawns. Cut large prawns into 2–3 pieces.

Wash, drain and finely shred the lettuce and place a small amount in each cocktail glass. Add the prepared shellfish, coat with Cocktail Sauce and top each with 1 teaspoon of caviar.

To decorate, cut into the white of the lemon wedge and set this on the edge of the glass. Place a sprig of parsley beside the lemon wedge inside the glass and serve with triangles of buttered bread.

Serves 4

HONEYED SEAFOOD

250 g seafood sticks, cut
   into 2 cm lengths
250 g uncooked prawns
   cut into 2 cm lengths
250 g boneless fish fillets
   cut into 2 cm cubes
seasoned cornflour
   (cornstarch)

oil for deep-frying
1½ tablespoons oil
3 tablespoons honey
1–2 tablespoons toasted
   sesame seeds
shallot flowers and lemon
   twists, to garnish

BATTER

1 cup self-raising flour
½ teaspoon salt
¼ teaspoon pepper

1¼ cups cold water
1 egg, beaten

To make batter sift flour, salt and pepper into a basin, then add water and beaten egg and blend.

Lightly coat the seafood with seasoned cornflour, dip in batter and deep-fry about 6 pieces at a time, until golden. Heat 1½ tablespoons oil in clean pan, stir in honey, add the cooked seafood and toss to coat each piece thoroughly with the honey mixture. Sprinkle with sesame seeds and serve garnished with small shallot flowers and lemon twists.

Serves 4–6

31

DEEP-FRIED CHEESE SCALLOPS

*½ cup fresh
breadcrumbs,
seasoned with salt,
freshly ground pepper,
garlic and thyme*
*2 egg whites at room
temperature*
250 g cheese, grated
*1 teaspoon
Worcestershire sauce*
*18 scallops, fresh, or
frozen and thawed*
oil for deep-frying
*1 cup fresh Chilli
Tomato Sauce (see
recipe)*
*lemon wedges and
parsley sprigs, to
garnish*

Beat egg whites until stiff. Gently fold in seasoned breadcrumbs, grated cheese and Worcestershire sauce.

Mould 1 tablespoon of the mixture around each scallop to form balls and deep-fry in oil heated to 162°C (325°F) for 5 minutes. Drain well on absorbent paper.

To serve, place 3 scallops on a small plate, spoon over a little Chilli Tomato Sauce and garnish with lemon wedges and sprigs of parsley.

Serves 6

REMOVING SCALLOPS FROM THE SHELL

You may prefer to use fresh scallops in the shell. They will be tightly closed, so you need a little help to open them. Place the shells under a pre-heated hotplate or in the oven for a few seconds. They will open so that the scallop meat can be carefully removed with a small knife. Wash them thoroughly and remove the trails leaving only the white scallop and the curved red roe. Discard the rest.

SEAFOOD NEWBURG

Seafood Newburg is a flexible dish that can be served in pastry cases, a pre-cooked flan case, individual fish-shaped vol-au-vents or with rice.

*2 cups prepared seafood
(scallops, prawns,
lobster)*
40 g butter
½ teaspoon paprika
2 tablespoons sherry
4 large egg yolks
1 cup cream
¼ teaspoon salt
freshly ground pepper
ground nutmeg

If you are using fresh, raw seafood, gently poach it in stock for 5 minutes, or until just cooked. Then cut seafood into 2 cm pieces and set aside.

Melt butter in the top of a double saucepan, add paprika and heat thoroughly, stirring in the sherry.

Beat egg yolks and stir in the cream, adding this to the sherry mixture and stirring until a creamy sauce forms. Do not boil.

Add seasonings and nutmeg and fold in seafood just before serving.

Serves 4–6

LOBSTER MOUSSE WITH DILL MAYONNAISE

*350 g cooked lobster
meat*
1 teaspoon salt
*1 teaspoon freshly
ground white pepper*
*4 eggs
plus 1 extra egg white*
40 g butter
3¼ cups cream

DILL MAYONNAISE

1½ cups mayonnaise   *½ bunch dill*

Cut lobster meat into 2 cm cubes and puree with salt and pepper. Add eggs plus the extra egg white and continue to puree until thoroughly blended. Cool in refrigerator for about 30 minutes.

Brush the inside of 6–8 souffle dishes with softened butter to coat lightly. Add cream to the lobster puree and mix together well, then spoon the mixture into souffle dishes and place in a large baking dish.

Fill baking dish so that the water level is halfway up the outside of the souffle dishes. Bake at 200°C (400°F) for 30 minutes.

To unmould, place a spatula across the top of each souffle dish, turn it over, allowing the juice to drain off before removing the mousse.

Blend mayonnaise and dill in food processor and serve with the individual souffles.

Serves 6–8

Deep-fried Cheese Scallops

CALAMARI WITH SNOW PEAS

500 g prepared calamari
   (squid), hoods
200 g snow peas
   (mangetout), fresh or
   frozen
⅓ cup stock
½ teaspoon sugar
1 teaspoon soy sauce
1 slice fresh root ginger,
   chopped finely

2 tablespoons oil
½ cup sliced bamboo
   shoot
2 shallots (spring onions,
   scallions), cut into
   2 cm lengths
1 teaspoon cornflour
   (cornstarch)
2 teaspoons water

Split each squid hood in half and cut into 2.5 cm
squares. Stem and blanch snow peas if using fresh
ones. Combine stock, sugar and soy sauce and set
aside.

Stir-fry the squid and ginger in oil for about 1 minute, then add bamboo shoots and shallots and stir-fry
for another 30 seconds. Blend in the stock mixture
and bring to the boil, adding the snow peas just to
heat through.

Thicken by stirring in cornflour blended in water,
then serve on individual dishes or in scallop shells.

Serves 4–6

Pan-fried Squid with Snow Peas

SALMON PATE

250 g fresh salmon or
   trout fillets
½ cup fish stock
½ cup dry white wine
280 g unsalted butter
125 g smoked salmon
3 tablespoons cream

salt to taste
freshly ground white
   pepper
freshly ground nutmeg
sprigs fresh dill and
   lemon twists for
   garnishing

Bring fillets slowly to the boil with fish stock and
wine, skim, then simmer gently until just tender.
Allow fillets to cool in the liquid, pick out skin and
bones, cut fish into small pieces and set aside. Boil
poaching liquid until it is reduced by half, then cool
and add 1 tablespoon of the liquid to the fillets.

Cut smoked salmon into small pieces and saute for
1–2 minutes in 30 g butter. Stir in cream, salt, pepper
and nutmeg. Cool, and blend adding the remaining
butter cut into knobs. When consistency is paste-like,
combine with the very small pieces of poached fish.

Serve at room temperature in small pate pots or
dishes. Garnish each with sprig of fresh dill and a
lemon twist.

Serves 6

SMOKED SALMON QUICHE

125 g thinly sliced
   smoked salmon

PASTRY

2 cups flour
½ teaspoon salt
125 g butter

1 egg yolk
1 tablespoon iced water

CUSTARD

300 mL cream
4 egg yolks

salt, cayenne and grated
   nutmeg, to taste

Sift flour and salt into a basin. Cut butter into small
cubes and rub into flour until the mixture resembles
fine breadcrumbs. Make a well in the centre, add the
egg yolk and water to make the pastry. Handle as
little and as lightly as possible to keep it cool and
manageable. Cover with plastic wrap and chill 30
minutes.

Roll out pastry and line 1 or more lightly greased
pie plates or quiche dishes.

Plaited Sole Fillets

Blend custard ingredients together and pour into pastry shell. Lightly float the salmon slices over the surface. With a teaspoon, carefully spoon some of the custard over the salmon but do not let the slices sink.

Bake in a pre-heated oven at 180°C (360°F) for 40–45 minutes. Let the quiche stand about 4 minutes before serving.

Serves 6–8

PLAITED SOLE FILLETS

6 fresh sole fillets, about 250 g each
½ cup seasoned flour
3 eggs, beaten
1½ cups white breadcrumbs

oil for frying
6 lemon wedges, pips removed
Tartare Sauce (see recipe)

FRIED PARSLEY

oil for deep-frying

sprigs of fresh green parsley

Preheat oil for deep-frying. Make sure the parsley is dry before you deep-fry it. Trim off excess stalks.

Drop the parsley, 3 sprigs at a time, into hot oil. When the spattering subsides, remove parsley quickly, so that it does not brown, and drain well on absorbent paper.

The sprigs of fried parsley should be crisp and deep green. Set aside to garnish the Plaited Sole Fillets.

Remove any black and white skin from fillets and cut each lengthways into 3 pieces leaving 1 cm uncut at 1 end of each fillet. Plait each fillet and secure the end with a toothpick.

Lightly toss fillets in seasoned flour, dip in beaten egg and coat with breadcrumbs. Deep-fry fillets at 185°C (360°F).

Serve each garnished with fried parsley and lemon wedges and Tartare Sauce.

Serves 6

Poultry

Every culture and cuisine has a rich and imaginative source of poultry recipes, and most can be exquisitely adapted to suit a menu of starter courses.

A bird is, of course, ideally designed for sectioning or preparing in smaller portion sizes; the limbs, breasts or liver of larger birds provide a perfect serving while a single quail, part boned or whole, makes an impressive and unusual appetiser.

Poultry, though quite distinctively flavoured itself, can well accommodate strong, spicy or piquant sauces and marinades, and its texture adapts well to mousses, terrines, souffles and quenelles.

The delicate flesh tones make even a lightly sauteed breast of chicken an exciting proposition when carefully sliced and arranged with sauce, mousse or complementing vegetables and garnishes.

So long as care is taken not to undercook chicken or overcook the birds, such as duck, which should ideally be served with slightly pink flesh, it is difficult to imagine a more easily mastered, impressive and satisfying range of starters than those provided by poultry.

CHICKEN AND CASHEWS

2 whole chicken breasts
3 tablespoons peanut oil
freshly ground black
 pepper
2 tablespoons soy sauce
1 cup diced celery
1 cup fresh peas
½ cup chopped onion
365 g can champignons
 (button mushrooms)
1 cup chicken stock
2 tablespoons oyster
 sauce
1 tablespoon cornflour
 (cornstarch)
2 tablespoons water or
 sherry
½ cup toasted cashew
 nuts

Dice chicken breasts into 2 cm cubes and gently cook them in oil for 3 minutes. Add pepper, soy sauce, celery, peas, onions and champignons and cook another 2–3 minutes. Stir in chicken stock, cover and simmer for 6 minutes.

Blend oyster sauce, cornflour and water and stir into the mixture until it thickens. Add cashews and serve with fried rice or noodles.

Serves 4

Clockwise from top right: Braised Quail, Steamed Vegetables, Chicken Supreme with Grape Sauce

CHICKEN DIANE

4 chicken breast fillets
freshly ground black
    pepper
60 g butter
2 cloves garlic, crushed
2 tablespoons
    Worcestershire sauce
2 tablespoons brandy
2 tablespoons cream
2 tablespoons finely
    chopped parsley
tomato roses, to garnish

Season chicken fillets lightly with pepper. Melt butter in pan, add garlic. When sizzling, cook fillets 2 minutes on each side. Add Worcestershire sauce and cover pan, simmering chicken fillets over medium heat for 12 minutes, turning after 6 minutes.

Warm brandy in a small saucepan for 15–20 seconds, flame it then pour over the chicken. Stir in cream and parsley and serve garnished with small tomato roses.

Serves 4

CHICKEN SUPREME WITH GINGERED GRAPE SAUCE

8 chicken breast fillets
onion salt
freshly ground white
    pepper
40 g butter
1½ tablespoons ginger
    marmalade
½ teaspoon dried
    tarragon
½ cup sauterne
½ cup sour (dairy
    soured) cream
2 teaspoons cornflour
    (cornstarch)
2 tablespoons chicken
    stock
½ cup seedless black or
    green grapes
watercress, to garnish

Season fillets lightly with onion salt and white pepper. Melt butter in frying pan and gently brown breasts on each side over a medium heat. Then add marmalade, tarragon and sauterne, covering the pan and simmering for 15–20 minutes until the fillets are cooked. Set aside on a warm serving plate.

Make sauce by stirring cream into pan juices then blending in a cornflour and chicken stock mixture, bringing it to the boil until the liquid thickens. Strain the sauce and return it to a clean pan, adding grapes and reheating until it boils.

Serve the fillets with the sauce, garnished with sprigs of watercress.

Serves 8

YAKITORI

3 whole chicken breast
    fillets
8 shallots, (spring onions,
    scallions)
⅓ cup sake (Japanese
    wine) or dry sherry
2 tablespoons soy sauce
2 slices fresh root ginger,
    peeled, finely shredded
1 clove garlic, peeled and
    crushed

Cut each fillet into 2 cm cubes. Chop white of shallots into 2.5 cm lengths. Thread onto satay sticks, alternating chicken cubes with shallot pieces.

Blend sake, soy sauce, ginger and garlic and brush over chicken, allowing it to marinate for 15 minutes.

Yakitori can be grilled or cooked in lightly oiled pan. Cooking time is about 8–10 minutes. Turn and baste during cooking to ensure even browning. Serve with rice.

Serves 6

CHICKEN SOUFFLE ROLL

500 g spinach leaf
15 g butter
4 large eggs, separated
2 tablespoons Parmesan
    cheese

FILLING

15 g butter
1 onion, chopped
125 g mushrooms,
    chopped
2 tablespoons flour
½ cup milk
250 g cooked diced
    chicken
30 g cream cheese
2 tablespoons sour (dairy
    soured) cream
2 teaspoons mustard,
    Dijon style
pinch salt, pepper and
    nutmeg

Grease and line a Swiss roll tray with greaseproof paper. Gently cook spinach in butter in a covered pan for 5–6 minutes until it wilts, then cool and chop it roughly. Puree the spinach, stir in egg yolks and season.

Fold stiffly beaten egg whites into the mixture with a metal spoon then spread over the prepared tray and sprinkle with Parmesan cheese. Bake at 200°C (400°F) for about 12 minutes or until firm to touch.

Gently sweat onions and mushrooms in butter until tender, add flour and cook for 1 minute without browning. Blend in milk to make sauce, then add

Chicken Souffle Roll

chicken, cream cheese and sour cream and cook until cheese melts. Season the mixture with mustard, salt, pepper and nutmeg.

Spread cooled filling over souffle. Roll up from the longest side with the aid of the greaseproof paper, arrange on serving platter.

Serves 6–8

CHICKEN MOUSSE

3½ tablespoons chopped
  onion
15 g butter
1¾ cups chicken stock
1 tablespoon gelatine
¼ cup dry white wine
500 g steamed chicken
  breast

60 g chicken liver pate
3 tablespoons Madeira
salt and pepper
pinch ground mace or
  nutmeg
300 mL thickened cream
  (double cream),
  whipped

CHAUDFROID SAUCE

2 cups Bechamel Sauce
  or Sauce Veloute (see
  recipes)

2 tablespoons gelatine
2–3 tablespoons cream

Saute onions in butter until tender. Blend gelatine into white wine and hot stock, beating until it dissolves.

Puree onions and gelatine mixture with chopped chicken breast, liver pate, Madeira and seasonings to taste.

Pour into a bowl and chill until almost set then fold in whipped cream.

Spoon mousse into individual pate pots or mould, cover and chill until set. Unmould onto a serving plate and chill while preparing Chaudfroid Sauce.

Soak gelatine in ¼ cup cold water. Bring Bechamel Sauce to the boil, remove from heat, add gelatine and stir until dissolved. Strain sauce through a sieve. When cool, add enough cream to enhance the colour.

Chill the sauce until it reaches the consistency of an egg white, then carefully spoon over mousse to give an even coating. Refrigerate until set.

Serves 6

CHICKEN QUENELLES

250 g chicken fillets
3 large egg whites
2 tablespoons cream
¼ teaspoon salt

pinch white pepper
1 litre rich chicken stock
strips of red capsicum
  (pepper), to garnish

Dice chicken breast and blend to a fine mince consistency with egg whites. Add cream, salt and pepper and blend.

Bring chicken stock to a gentle simmer. To cook the quenelles, use 2 teaspoons, dipped into cold

Chicken Gougere

water. Spoon out the mixture with one spoon and use the other to slide it into simmering stock. Repeat until chicken is all used. The quenelles are cooked when they rise to the surface of the stock.

Lift out quenelles with a slotted spoon and place them into cold stock or water. They can be stored in refrigerator until you need them.

To serve, reheat them in Sauce Supreme or Sauce Aurora (see recipes). Allow about 8 quenelles per serve. Garnish with very thin strips of red capsicum.

Serves 4

CHICKEN ROULADES WITH GREEN PEPPERCORN SAUCE

3 whole chicken breasts,
  skinned and boned
salt and white pepper
1½ tablespoons lemon
  juice, strained

60 g butter
sliced kiwi fruit, to
  garnish (optional)

GREEN PEPPERCORN SAUCE

3 tablespoons canned
  green peppercorns
3 egg yolks
3 tablespoons cream

3 tablespoons sour (dairy
  soured) cream
2 teaspoons French
  mustard

Lightly pound each breast with a meat mallet and season with salt, pepper and lemon juice. Roll each breast lengthways and fasten with poultry skewers or strong toothpicks.

Melt 40 g butter in frying pan, add the chicken roulades, cover and cook over moderate heat for

15–20 minutes, turning the roulades during cooking. Remove chicken from pan, set aside and reduce pan juices.

Rinse peppercorns in warm water. Heat remaining butter in saucepan, add peppercorns and cook for 1–2 minutes.

Combine egg yolks, cream, sour cream and mustard. Add to peppercorns along with pan juices. Stir over low heat until sauce thickens. If sauce is too thick, thin down with chicken stock or white wine. Do not boil.

Serve chicken with sauce garnished with sliced kiwi fruit.

Serves 6

Sweet and Sour Deep-fried Chicken Wings

SWEET AND SOUR CHICKEN WINGS

12 chicken wings	oil for deep frying
2 eggs, beaten lightly	2 slices fresh root ginger
½ cup cornflour (cornstarch), seasoned	

SWEET AND SOUR SAUCE

¾ cup water	¼ cup cold water
½ cup sugar	2 tablespoons tomato
½ cup white vinegar	sauce
1 tablespoon cornflour (cornstarch)	

Cut bony tips from each chicken wing. Dip each wing in beaten egg, then coat with cornflour. Heat oil with ginger, and when ginger browns, deep-fry 2 or 3 wings at a time until golden. Drain well, keep warm.

Bring water to the boil, stir in sugar and dissolve. Add vinegar and cook for 1 minute. Blend the cornflour, water and tomato sauce and stir into sauce to thicken.

Add the chicken wings and gently heat through.

Serves 4–6

SPICED CHICKEN DRUMSTICKS

16 chicken drumsticks	¼ cup lemon or lime
1 cup natural yoghurt	juice, strained
¼ teaspoon turmeric	sliced mango (in season),
1 teaspoon ground ginger	to garnish
2 cloves garlic, finely chopped	lemon or lime wedges, to garnish
1 teaspoon salt	
½–1 teaspoon chilli or cayenne pepper	

Remove skin and cut each drumstick 2 or 3 times halfway to the bone so marinade can penetrate. Cover the chicken thickly with a mixture of natural yoghurt, turmeric, ground ginger, garlic, salt, chilli or cayenne pepper and lemon (or lime) juice and refrigerate for 6–8 hours, turning occasionally.

Lift drumsticks from the marinade, drain briefly then bake in a well-greased dish for 40–50 minutes at 200°C (400°F). Turn and baste with marinade several times during cooking. Serve arranged on a platter with sliced mango and lemon wedges.

Serves 8

CHICKEN AND ASPARAGUS CREPES

12 pre-cooked crepes (see recipe)
60 g butter
1 small onion, chopped
125 g mushrooms, sliced
3 tablespoons flour
⅔ cup chicken stock
½ cup milk or cream
2 cups diced, cooked chicken
250 g asparagus spears, cooked and diced
⅓ cup Parmesan cheese
pinch fresh thyme
½ teaspoon salt
freshly ground pepper
½ cup grated cheese

Melt butter in frying pan and add onions and mushrooms, cooking gently until tender. Mix in flour and cook for 1 minute without browning. Add chicken stock and milk, stirring until the sauce boils and thickens.

Remove from heat and stir in diced chicken, asparagus, Parmesan cheese, thyme, salt and pepper and leave to cool.

Place a little filling along the middle of each crepe and roll up. Arrange crepe 'cannelloni' in a single layer in shallow oblong dish, cover with aluminium foil and bake at 185°C (370°F) for 20 minutes to heat through. Remove aluminium foil, sprinkle with cheese and bake uncovered until the cheese melts.

Allow 2 crepes per serving.

Serves 6

CHICKEN GOUGERE
CHOUX PASTRY

1¼ cups water
60 g butter
1 cup flour
3 x 55 g eggs
1 cup grated tasty cheese
pinch cayenne pepper
1 egg, beaten
¼ cup Parmesan cheese

FILLING

20 g butter
4 shallots (spring onions, scallions), chopped
2 slices ham, diced
¼ cup button mushrooms, sliced
1 tablespoon flour
⅔ cup rich chicken stock
2 cups cooked white chicken, diced
1 tomato, skinned, seeded and chopped
¼ cup sour (dairy soured) cream
¼ cup tasty cheese
salt and pepper

TOPPING

3 tablespoons buttered breadcrumbs

Make choux pastry by bringing water to boil with the butter. Remove from heat, add all the flour at once and beat vigorously until the mixture is smooth. Return to heat and continue stirring until the dough leaves the sides of the saucepan cleanly. Spread out flat to cool. Place in a bowl and beat, adding the eggs 1 at a time and beating well after each addition. The dough should be smooth and glossy.

Blend cheese and cayenne pepper into choux pastry. Grease a rectangular ovenproof dish and pipe or spoon choux mixture around the edge. Glaze the pastry with beaten egg and sprinkle with Parmesan cheese.

Gently saute shallots and ham in butter for 1 minute. Stir in mushrooms and flour and cook another minute. Gradually add stock, stirring until boiling, then remove from the heat.

Fold in chicken, tomato, sour cream, cheese and seasonings, then spoon into the centre of ovenproof dish. Sprinkle with buttered breadcrumbs and bake in centre of oven at 200°C (400°F) for 35–40 minutes.

Serve cut into wedges.

Serves 4

CHICKEN AVOCADO SUPREME

1 onion
½ stalk celery
2 bay leaves
6 peppercorns
½ cup white wine
1 litre cold water
1 x 1.7 kg chicken
80 g butter
⅓ cup flour
4 cups chicken stock
2 egg yolks, beaten
freshly ground black pepper
2 medium-sized avocados
6 vol-au-vent cases
2 tablespoons diced pimiento, to garnish

Bring onion, celery, bay leaves, peppercorns, wine and water to boil in a large saucepan, add chicken and simmer until tender. When cooked, skin and bone the chicken and cut it into 2 cm pieces.

Melt butter, stirring in flour until smooth, then pour in stock and stir until it boils.

Blend 2 tablespoons of sauce into the egg yolks and stir into remaining sauce, seasoning with pepper to taste, and finally adding the chicken.

Reheat gently. Peel and dice avocados and fold into sauce just before serving. Spoon into warmed vol-au-vent cases, sprinkle with pimiento and serve.

Serves 6

Chicken Livers Veronique

CHICKEN LIVERS VERONIQUE

750 g chicken livers
2 tablespoons chopped
   shallots
60 g butter
1 tablespoon fruit juice
3 tablespoons white wine
3 tablespoons chicken
   stock

1½ cups seedless grapes
4–6 tablespoons sour
   (dairy soured) cream
finely chopped parsley,
   to garnish

SEASONED FLOUR

flour
freshly ground pepper
salt

¼ teaspoon ground
   ginger

Rinse chicken livers, pat dry and dust with seasoned flour. Saute shallots and livers in butter over a medium heat for 6–8 minutes. Pour in fruit juice, white wine and stock and bring to the boil. Then add grapes and reduce the heat, covering the pan and cooking for 3 minutes. Stir in sour cream and reheat gently. Serve sprinkled with finely chopped parsley.

Serves 6

PATE MAISON

1 onion, chopped
1 clove garlic, crushed
sprig fresh thyme
sprig parsley
sprig chervil
60 g butter
250 g chicken livers,
   cleaned

salt and pepper
125 g fat pork, roughly
   chopped
125 g lean pork, roughly
   chopped
6 bacon rashers

Gently cook onion, garlic and herbs in butter for 1–2 minutes, then add livers diced into 2 cm pieces, and cook gently for about 1 minute. Cool, then season and puree with the pork.

Line a terrine with rashers of bacon and spoon in the meat mixture, covering it with more bacon rashers. Stand the terrine in a baking dish half full of water and bake at 180° (360°F) for 1 hour. Cool, then refrigerate until firm. When chilled, slice pate and serve on lettuce leaves, accompanied by triangles of toast.

Serves 8

43

Smoked Turkey with Pawpaw

SMOKED TURKEY WITH PAWPAW

1 medium-sized pawpaw
12 thin slices smoked
   turkey breast

lime wedges and
   watercress sprigs, to
   garnish

CRANBERRY MAYONNAISE

6–8 tablespoons well-
flavoured mayonnaise
blended with

3 tablespoons cranberry
   sauce

Peel pawpaw, cut in half and remove seeds. Cut each half lengthways into thirds.

Arrange 2 thin slices of turkey on each portion of pawpaw. Serve on individual plates, garnished with lime wedges and watercress sprigs.

Serve Cranberry Mayonnaise separately.

Serves 6

TURKEY PATE

2 bacon rashers
1 onion, finely chopped
375 g cooked turkey,
   plain or smoked,
   minced
2 tablespoons cream

1 tablespoon French
   mustard
1 tablespoon brandy
60 g butter
salt and pepper
parsley sprigs to garnish

Remove rind from bacon, chop and gently fry until fat runs, then remove and set aside. Sweat onion in bacon fat until transparent. Combine turkey with bacon, onion, cream, mustard and brandy, mixing thoroughly. Stir in butter until smooth, seasoning to taste. Pack into pate pots or small dishes and garnish with parsley sprigs.

Serves 4

SMOKED TURKEY QUICHE

You can substitute the same amount of your favourite meat from the delicatessen counter for the smoked turkey.

1 sheet ready-made puff
   or short crust pastry
25 g butter
1 tablespoon finely
   chopped onion
250 g smoked turkey,
   chopped
3 eggs

½ cup cream
½ cup milk
1 teaspoon flour
pinch cayenne
pinch dried marjoram
1 medium-sized tomato,
   peeled and finely sliced
parsley sprigs, to garnish

Lightly grease a 20 cm diameter fluted flan tin and line with pastry.

Saute onion in 5 g butter until transparent then sprinkle over the pastry with the chopped turkey. Whisk eggs, beating in the cream, milk, flour, cayenne, marjoram and 20 g butter melted. Spoon into pastry case and decorate with tomato slices.

Bake at 200°C (400°F) for 10 minutes, then lower heat to 180°C (360°F) and continue to bake for another 20 minutes until custard is set.

Serves 4–6

Note: If you are freezing a quiche, slightly underbake it. When you want to use it, thaw the frozen quiche and bake it at 180°C (360°F) for 15 minutes before serving.

Breast of Duckling with Apricot Sauce

BREAST OF DUCKLING WITH APRICOT SAUCE

1 x 3 kg duckling
1 bay leaf
few celery leaves
10 black peppercorns
few sprigs parsley

1 small onion, sliced
3 tablespoons white wine
mustard cress or
*   watercress to garnish*

APRICOT SAUCE

¾ cup dried apricots
salt and freshly ground
*   pepper*

juice of ½ lemon
1 tablespoon brandy

Dislocate the wing and leg joints of the duck and cut off. Cut off the wing tips and reserve. Keep the wings and legs for another recipe. Cut the breast away from the backbone and leave whole, then place the wing tips and backbone in a pan, cover with water and bring to the boil. Lift off any foam, then add the bayleaf, celery leaves, peppercorns, parsley, onion and wine, and simmer, partially covered, for 1–1½ hours.

Strain and reserve 2 cups of the stock to soak the apricots in for 1–2 hours. Cook the apricots until tender and puree them. Taste and adjust the seasoning with salt, pepper and lemon juice. Add brandy to the Apricot Sauce and stir. If the sauce is a little thick, thin it down with extra stock.

Prick the duck breast with a skewer, season lightly with salt and place in a pan and roast in a moderately hot oven 190°C (375°F) for 10 minutes then reduce the heat to 180°C (350°F) and roast for another 20 minutes or until cooked when tested. Remove the breast and let it cool to room temperature. Carefully peel off all the skin and slice flesh neatly.

Pour ⅓ cup of sauce into 4 plates and arrange overlapping slices of duck and skin on top. Garnish with mustard cress or watercress and serve any remaining sauce separately.

Serves 4
Note: The stock and sauce can be prepared in advance. The duck can be served warm or cool.

45

Game Birds

A wide variety of game birds are aged before they are sold. This means that before they are plucked, they have been hung for a few days to ensure tenderness and that distinctive 'game' flavour. Specialised poultry shops also offer frozen dressed game right throughout the year.

Game can make a delicious starter. To prevent the bird from drying out while it is roasting, spread a thin layer of pork back fat over the breast section. While the bird cooks, this will melt, basting the flesh throughout cooking time.

Roasting game can be served on a croute (round of fried bread) with toasted French bread spread with game forcemeat and watercress sprigs for a garnish. Serve any gravy or bread sauce separately.

ROAST PHEASANT ITALIAN STYLE

1 large pheasant, prepared for roasting	1¼ cups fresh chicken stock
1–2 strips of pork back fat	250 g macaroni
1 cup white wine	1 cup grated Parmesan cheese
4 ripe tomatoes	salt and pepper

Place pheasant into roasting dish and cover breast and drumsticks with strips of pork fat. Pour over white wine, cover and roast (as for other poultry), basting occasionally.

Peel and slice tomatoes, add to the stock and bring to boil. Add the macaroni and simmer until cooked. Fold in Parmesan cheese and seasoning and continue cooking for a few minutes.

Cut pheasant into serving pieces and arrange on a bed of macaroni. Serve garnished with watercress.

Serves 4–6

GUINEA FOWL WITH ORANGE SAUCE

Originating in Africa, the guinea fowl is now bred around the world. The guinea hen is, however, the more tender bird and is sized right for two portions.

1 guinea hen	grated zest and juice of 1 orange and 1 lemon
cup dry white wine	1 tablespoon flour
110 g butter	1 cup chicken stock
2½ tablespoons walnut or olive oil	
1 teaspoon chopped fresh thyme	

Cut guinea hen in ½, lengthways and place in a deep-sided dish. Combine the wine, oil, 60 g butter, thyme, zest and juice of orange and lemon and bring to boil. Pour marinade over guinea hen and leave to cool — about 30 minutes.

Reserving marinade, pat bird dry and brown well in remaining butter in frying pan. Transfer to a baking dish and bake at 220°C (425°F) for 15 minutes. Arrange portions on a serving plate and keep warm (turn oven off and leave door open).

Stir flour into butter in frying pan for 1 minute then gradually add stock, stirring constantly. Add 1 cup of marinade and boil until sauce reduces and thickens. Spoon over guinea hen and serve or serve separately.

Serves 2

GRILLED QUAIL WITH MUSTARD SAUCE

8 quails	100 g butter
100 g Dijon mustard	1 tablespoon olive oil
½ teaspoon cracked black pepper	4 rashers bacon

Cut the quails in ½ along the breast bone and spread open so that they lie flat.

Combine the mustard, pepper, butter and oil to form a smooth paste. Spread over the backs of each quail. Cut the bacon in ½ and place a rasher on each quail.

Preheat griller and cook the quails, cut side down, basting occasionally with juice from the birds. Turn the quails once during the 8–10 minutes of cooking time. Serve immediately.

Serves 4

Braised Quail with Ginger Honey Sauce

BRAISED QUAIL WITH GINGER HONEY SAUCE

8 quail
1 clove garlic, finely
   chopped
4 slices fresh ginger,
   peeled and finely
   shredded

2-3 tablespoons oil
½ cup dry sherry
2 tablespoons honey
2 tablespoons soy sauce
½ teaspoon salt

JULIENNE VEGETABLES

½ red capsicum
   (pepper), seeded
½ green capsicum
   (pepper), seeded

4 snow peas (mangetout)
   remove stems
½ carrot, peeled

Truss each quail with white string so it retains its shape while cooking.

Gently fry garlic and ⅓ ginger in a large pan for 1-2 minutes. Reduce heat, add the quail, brown lightly, then drain off excess oil.

Combine sherry, honey, soy sauce and salt and pour over quail. Simmer, covered for 15 minutes, turning each quail halfway through cooking time.

To serve, remove string, transfer quail to serving platter and keep warm. Strain sauce, then reheat and add the remaining ginger. Correct seasoning then coat each quail evenly with sauce. Garnish with strips of blanched Julienne Vegetables.

To prepare vegetables, cut into fine matchstick lengths, blanch in boiling water then drain and refresh.

Serves 4

Meat

With the modern trend away from hearty servings, starter-sized portions are increasingly popular. In addition, bonnes bouches of, say Pork Crepinettes with Butter Fried Apples (*see recipe*) seem infinitely more tempting than several slices of roast pork with traditional apple sauce and the usual trappings of boiled or roast vegetables.

The key to successful meat entrees is creating interest and impact. A Fricassee of Kidneys, Sweetbreads and Spinach (*see recipe*) offers a variety of textures and taste while Lamb Medallions en Croute (*see recipe*) are stylish, simple and tasty. Complementary garnishes and a crisply cooked arrangement of vegetables will complete the picture and create an irresistible appetiser.

FRICASSEE OF KIDNEYS AND SWEETBREADS WITH SPINACH

2 veal kidneys
2 sets veal sweetbreads
1 litre cold water
500 g English spinach
75 g butter, melted
2 tablespoons oil
2 shallots (spring onions, scallions), finely chopped
¼ cup dry white wine
1 chicken stock cube
dash paprika
300 mL thickened cream (double cream)
salt and pepper
chopped parsley and lemon twists, to garnish

Trim and remove fat and skin from the kidneys with scissors. Cut them in half lengthways and remove the veins. Soak kidneys and sweetbreads in separate bowls of water for 30 minutes. Drain and soak another 30 minutes in salted water.

Simmer sweetbreads for 5 minutes in 1 litre of water then drain and peel away any membrane or fatty tissue. Cut both kidneys and sweetbreads into bite-sized pieces.

Slice stalks from spinach and cook leaves in boiling salted water for 1 minute, drain and press out excess water. Spread out spinach leaves in a shallow dish and pour over the melted butter, reserving about 2 tablespoons.

Use the reserved butter to gently fry the kidneys and sweetbreads until they are golden. Lift out meat and set aside. Heat oil and add shallots and white wine and simmer until reduced by half. Add stock cube, paprika, cream, salt and pepper and simmer for 5 minutes then heat the kidneys and sweetbreads through in this mixture.

Arrange the spinach leaves on individual plates, spoon a serving of kidneys and sweetbreads onto each and garnish with parsley and a lemon twist.

Serves 4

Fricasee of Kidneys and Sweetbreads with Spinach

CRUMBED LEMON LIVER

1 kg calf's liver
1-2 eggs
salt
flour
fine breadcrumbs

¾ cup butter
juice of 1 lemon
1½ teaspoons sugar
½ red capsicum
    (pepper), thinly sliced

Soak liver in cold water for 2 hours, changing the water twice, then drain and remove any fatty pieces. Slice liver finely.

Beat eggs. Combine flour and salt in a separate bowl. Coat liver in flour then egg and breadcrumbs, and fry in butter until browned on both sides. Transfer to a serving platter.

Slowly heat lemon juice with the sugar, stirring until the sugar dissolves. Pour over liver and serve garnished with blanched strips of capsicum.

Serves 6

BRAINS WITH PARMESAN

1 set brains (6 sheep
    brains to 1 set)
1 onion, peeled
2 cloves
juice 1 lemon
salt
¼ teaspoon thyme
1 bay leaf
1 litre cold water

12 thin slices bread
1⅔ cups Parmesan
    cheese
125 g butter, melted
3 tablespoons coarse-
    grain mustard
6 lemon slices and
    watercress sprigs, to
    garnish

Soak brains in cold water for 2 hours, changing the water 2 or 3 times.

Bring the onion, cloves, lemon juice, salt, thyme, bay leaf and 1 litre of water to the boil, then simmer for 30 minutes. Remove the bay leaf and allow the stock to cool. Place the brains in the cooled stock and bring slowly back to the boil.

As soon as the stock boils, lift out the brains and remove any membrane on them. Now return brains to the stock and simmer for 20 minutes. Drain carefully, reserving the stock and allowing the brains to cool. Add mustard to the stock.

Remove crusts from bread, reserve and toast each slice. Crumb the crusts and combine with Parmesan

Place the toast in an ovenproof dish with 1 brain on each slice. Spoon over melted butter and small portion of mustard stock. Sprinkle with Parmesan cheese and crumbs and bake for 10 minutes at 200°C (400°F).

Serve toast and brains together on individual plates garnished with lemon slices and watercress.

Serves 6

DEEP-FRIED CREPES WITH VEAL AND MUSHROOM

12 pre-cooked crepes (see
    recipe)
30 g butter
1 tablespoon oil
8 shallots (spring onions,
    scallions), chopped
250 g mushrooms, sliced
    thinly
4 tablespoons brandy
salt
freshly ground black
    pepper
300 mL cream, beaten
    with 2 egg yolks

250 g veal mince, cooked
¼ teaspoon garam
    marsala
3 tablespoons cornflour
    (cornstarch) mixed
    with 3 tablespoons
    water
3 cups oil for deep-frying
2 eggs beaten with 1
    tablespoon water (egg
    wash)
1 cup fresh breadcrumbs
oil for deep-frying

Heat butter and oil in frying pan and cook shallots and mushrooms for 1 minute. Add brandy, salt and pepper and cook another minute. Now stir in the cream and egg yolks, veal mince and garam marsala. Add the cornflour and water and cook until the mixture thickens, stirring continuously. Chill in refrigerator.

When chilled, place 1 tablespoon in the centre of each crepe, fold over 1 end, fold in 2 sides and then fold over to form a parcel.

Dip each parcel in egg wash and breadcrumbs and fry until golden in hot oil. Drain and serve hot with a Hollandaise or Tomato Sauce (see recipes)

Serves 4–6

Deep-fried Crepes with Veal and Mushroom

VEAL SCALLOPS BAKED IN MILK

6 veal steaks
seasoned flour
1 tablespoon oil
30 g butter
¼ cup milk
¼ cup cream
1 tablespoon French
  mustard
salt

freshly ground black
  pepper
2 tablespoons chopped
  parsley
125 g button mushrooms
1 cup julienne carrots
  and 1 cup finely
  shredded spinach, to
  garnish

Place veal steaks between 2 sheets plastic wrap and gently beat with a rolling pin to tenderise. Dust veal lightly with seasoned flour, brown on both sides in oil and place in an ovenproof dish.

Melt butter in frying pan then add the milk, cream, mustard, salt, pepper and parsley. Cook, stirring continually, until the sauce thickens. Arrange mushrooms on top of the veal steaks, pour over the sauce and bake for 10 minutes at 200°C (400°F).

Serve veal with sauce and mushrooms, garnished with blanched julienne carrots and finely shredded spinach.

Serves 4–6

MIXED MEAT GOUGERE

2 kidneys
250 g topside, thinly
  sliced
60 g mushrooms, sliced
60 g ham, diced
90 g butter
250 g tasty cheese, grated
3 tablespoons cornflour
  (cornstarch)

1 cup milk
½ teaspoon salt
freshly ground black
  pepper
1 cup water
1 cup flour
2 eggs, beaten
parsley sprigs, to garnish

Prepare kidneys as described in Fricassee of Kidneys and Sweetbreads (see recipe). Fry kidneys, topside, mushrooms and ham in 30 g butter until brown then set aside.

Combine cheese and cornflour in a saucepan (off the heat). Gradually add the milk and heat, stirring constantly. Add salt and pepper, then meat mixture and set aside.

Bring water and 60 g butter to the boil, remove from heat and add flour, stirring vigorously.

Return saucepan to the heat and stir until the mixture is smooth and comes away from the sides of the saucepan. Cool slightly, then add the eggs, beating

well. Spoon into 4 individual souffle dishes, spreading the mixture round the sides of the dish and leaving a hollow in the centre for meat filling.

Place an equal amount of filling in each dish and bake for 30 minutes at 200°C (400°F).

Garnish with parsley and serve with a salad.

Serves 4

LAMB MEDALLIONS EN CROUTE

2 kg leg lamb, boned and
  trimmed
6 cloves garlic
salt, pepper
2 sprigs fresh rosemary
2 tablespoons oil
6 sheets frozen puff
  pastry, thawed
6 slices ham
30 g butter
6 shallots (spring onions,
  scallions), chopped
375 g mushrooms,
  chopped
salt and pepper
½ cup brandy

⅔ cup sour (dairy
  soured) cream
2 tablespoons finely
  chopped walnuts
2 tablespoons cornflour
  (cornstarch) mixed
  with 2 tablespoons
  water
½ teaspoon thyme
2 eggs beaten with 1
  teaspoon milk (egg
  wash)
¼ cup sesame seeds
watercress and 12 cherry
  tomatoes, to serve

Cut lamb lengthways and open out to an even thickness, then roll up and tie with string. Stud with garlic and season with salt and pepper.

Put rosemary and oil in a baking pan with the lamb, cover with foil and roast for 2 hours at 160°C (325°F). When cooked, let lamb rest 15 minutes then carve in 6 portions, removing string from each portion.

Place a slice of ham in the centre of each pastry sheet. Trim a 6 mm strip from each edge of pastry sheet.

Saute butter, shallots, mushrooms and seasonings for 2 minutes. Add brandy and simmer until liquid is reduced to half. Stir in sour cream, walnuts, cornflour mixture and thyme and cook until thickened. Cool slightly.

Place 1 portion of lamb on the ham and pastry, spread with a little walnut mixture, and roll up pastry and meat leaving the ends open. Tie the ends in a bon-bon shape, with pastry strips. Brush parcels with egg wash, sprinkle with sesame seeds and bake (seam side down) for 30 minutes at 200°C (400°F) or until

Lamb Medallions en Croute

the pastry is golden brown. Serve with watercress and cherry tomatoes.

Serves 6

PORK CREPINETTES WITH BUTTER-FRIED APPLES

375 g pork mince
375 g veal mince
375 beef suet, minced
3 cups fresh breadcrumbs
grated rind of lemon
1 teaspoon nutmeg
salt and pepper
½ tablespoon thyme
¼ tablespoon marjoram
thin sheets of pork back fat
2 cooking apples, peeled and sliced

Mix the meats, suet, breadcrumbs, lemon rind, seasonings and herbs well together.

With floured hands, roll portions of crepinette mixture into an oval shape, flatten lightly, then wrap in 20 cm square pork back fat and press it gently into place.

Fry crepinettes in small amount of oil, browning both sides, drain and serve with apple slices fried in butter.

Serves 6

53

SHREDDED PORK AND MUSHROOM TARTLETS

PASTRY

90 g butter
1 cup flour
salt

1 egg yolk
squeeze lemon juice

FILLING

60 g mushroom caps,
   halved
60 g can champignons
   (button mushrooms),
   halved
250 g pork steak,
   shredded
1 cup red wine
salt
freshly ground black

pepper
1 bay leaf
¼ cup leek rings
1 tablespoon finely
   chopped parsley
30 g butter
watercress sprigs and
   carrot straws, to
   garnish

Rub butter into flour and salt, blend in egg yolk and lemon juice to form a soft dough. Wrap and chill for 10 minutes in refrigerator then roll out and line 6 x 10 cm diameter quiche dishes. Prick base of pastry and bake blind for 15 minutes at 200°C (400°F) Carefully remove pastry case from container and cool while preparing the filling.

Marinate mushrooms, champignons and pork steak in red wine, salt, pepper and bay leaf for 10 minutes.

In a large pan, gently fry leek rings, parsley and butter. Drain meat and mushrooms, reserving marinade. Add meat and mushrooms to leeks and fry for 3 minutes, then add wine and seasonings. Bring to the boil, then simmer uncovered till filling reduces and thickens. Spoon pork and mushroom filling into pastry cases and serve garnished with watercress and carrot straws.

Serves 4–6

Shredded Pork and Mushroom Tartlets

COLD SLICED MEATS

A major charm of cold meat meals is that they can be prepared well in advance and thus ease the burden on the cook, allowing ample opportunity either to concentrate on a more complicated course or to relax with guests.

However, this does not infer that they are in any way a dull option. As entree dishes, cold meats can be spiced or served simply, with a tangy sauce. They have great visual potential in the form of terrines, or when set in aspic with the addition of bright garnishes.

Depending on the manner in which they are presented, cold meat dishes can be served as simple but epicurean picnic fare, eye-catching buffet appetisers or elevated into exotic and elegant dinner party dishes. The generally undemanding preparations can be compensated by extra efforts in the presentation.

Cold sliced meats are simply delicious served with mustard, fruit chutneys or any of the range of special sauces in the Sauce chapter of this book.

Individual Meat Plate with Smoked Turkey Breast, Mortadella, Proscuitto and Roast Beef

POTTED TONGUE AND VEAL PATE

250 g veal, minced
1 tablespoon brandy
250 g cooked tongue
60 g ham steak
¼ cup finely chopped
    leek
1 teaspoon prepared
    mustard

salt
freshly ground black
    pepper
½ teaspoon nutmeg
90 g butter, melted and
    cooled
orange twists, cucumber,
    crackers, to serve

Cook veal and brandy gently in a frying pan then puree veal and half the pan juices.

Add tongue, ham steak, leek, mustard, salt, pepper and nutmeg and blend until smooth, gradually adding the melted butter. Spoon into small pate pots and chill.

Garnish with orange twists and serve with cucumber sticks and crackers.

Serves 4–6

MIXED MEAT PATE

6 slices white bread,
  crusts removed
½ cup brandy
500 g chicken livers
2 eggs
4 shallots (spring onions,
  scallions), sliced
125 g bacon rashers, rind
  removed
500 g pork and veal
  mince
½ teaspoon ground
  allspice
1 teaspoon seasoning salt
freshly ground black
  pepper
1 teaspoon dried
  marjoram
6–8 bacon rashers extra,
  rind removed

Soak bread in brandy for 10 minutes. In the mean-time, clean and roughly chop the livers. Mince together with eggs, spring onions and bacon rashers, then add pork and veal mince, allspice, seasonings and marjoram and blend until the ingredients are just combined.

Line a 23 x 13 x 6 cm deep loaf tin with extra bacon and spoon mixture in, folding over bacon ends. Cover with foil and bake in baking dish half full of water at 180°C (360°F) for 1½ hours until pate has shrunk slightly from sides of the dish. Weight the pate and refrigerate until cold.

Serves 8–10

PATE-STUFFED BREAD

1 large loaf crusty French
  bread
500 g cream cheese
¼ cup beer
¼ cup chopped onion
¼ cup chopped parsley
¼ cup chopped radishes
1 tablespoon dry mustard
250 g liverwurst, cut into
  cubes

Slice off ends of bread and cut loaf vertically into 3 pieces. Pull out crumbly inside leaving only a 5 mm thick crusty shell. Crumble bread and bake at 180°C (360°F)° for 15 minutes.

Blend cheese until smooth, then stir in beer, onion, parsley, radishes and mustard. Fold in liverwurst and toasted crumbs. Pack into bread shells. Reassemble the loaf, wrap in foil and refrigerate for 4 hours or overnight. Slice thinly and serve.

Serves 6–8

RABBIT TERRINE

180 g prunes
red wine
1 kg rabbit legs or 2 kg
   whole rabbit
500 g belly of pork
250 g stewing veal

375 g bacon rashers, rind
   removed
3-4 whole juniper berries
1 teaspoon dried sage
1 teaspoon dried oregano
1 teaspoon ground mace

MARINADE

juice of 1 orange
3 tablespoons brandy
10 juniper berries,
   crushed
10 whole allspice,
   crushed

8 black peppercorns,
   crushed
4 bay leaves
1 teaspoon salt

Soak prunes in enough red wine to cover and leave them overnight. Remove flesh from rabbit and chop into small pieces, arrange in shallow dish and pour over combined marinade ingredients. Cover and refrigerate for 8 hours or overnight, turning occasionally.

Remove and discard rind from pork, and mince with veal.

Grease a 1 litre earthenware terrine. Arrange the bay leaves from the marinade on the bottom of terrine to form a pattern with the juniper berries. Place all but 2 bacon rashers on bottom and around sides of terrine.

Drain prunes and remove seeds; drain rabbit meat, reserving marinade. Arrange a layer of rabbit on the bacon, sprinkle over herbs and mace and a few prunes then follow with a layer of pork and veal mince, more herbs and mace, prunes, rabbit and so on until all ingredients are used up. Then strain the marinade and pour over. Place 2 bay leaves on top and cover with 2 remaining bacon rashers.

Cover terrine with greased foil and a lid, place in a pan of water and bake at 160°C (320°F) for 1½–2 hours until a skewer, inserted in the centre, comes out clean. Stand for 30 minutes then weight the terrine and leave for several hours or overnight.

To serve, dip terrine quickly in very hot water and turn out onto serving dish.

Serves 10–14

Mixed Meat Pate served with Cumberland Sauce (see recipes)

ARABIAN MEAT LOAF

2 kg minced lamb
1 egg, beaten
1 cup water
½ cup dried
  breadcrumbs
2 tablespoons lemon juice
2 tablespoons tomato
  paste
2 teaspoons garlic salt
freshly ground black

pepper
½ teaspoon ground
  cinnamon
½ teaspoon grated
  nutmeg
oil for brushing
¼ cup dried
  breadcrumbs for
  coating

BASTING SAUCE

¼ cup vinegar
¼ cup water

2 tablespoons tomato
  paste

Mince meat in food processor to a smooth paste. Blend with egg, water, breadcrumbs, lemon juice, tomato paste and seasonings until very smooth. Divide mixture in half and shape into 2 oblong rolls. Brush each with oil and coat with breadcrumbs and bake in shallow baking pan at 180°C (360°F) for 1 hour. As the meat loaf begins to brown, baste with sauce every 15 minutes. When cold slice thinly and serve.

Serves 8–10

Pesto-stuffed Veal

PESTO-STUFFED VEAL

½ cup firmly packed
  fresh basil leaves
2 cloves garlic, peeled
½ cup pine nuts
1 tablespoon tomato
  paste
¼ cup Parmesan cheese
1 tablespoon oil

100 g butter
1 cup fresh white
  breadcrumbs
2 kg boned loin of veal
½ cup chicken or veal
  stock
Mustard Sauce for
  serving, (see recipe)

Puree basil, garlic, pine nuts and tomato paste then add cheese.

Heat oil and 40 g butter, add breadcrumbs, toss until crumbs are well coated and combine with basil mixture.

Place veal, skin side down, on board and spread stuffing along one side. Roll veal flap over the stuffing and tie firmly with string at 2.5 cm intervals. Put veal on a lightly greased rack in baking dish and spread over the remaining butter. Pour stock into pan and bake at 200°C (400°F) for 15 minutes. Reduce heat to 150°C (300°F) and continue to cook for another 1½ hours until juices run clear when meat is pierced with a skewer. Baste every 15 minutes with pan juices to prevent veal from drying out. Cover with foil and refrigerate until cool. Serve with Mustard Sauce.

Serves 8

Arabian Meat Loaf

CORNETS DE JAMBON

12 slices ham or
   mortadella
20 g butter
1 tablespoon flour
¾ cup milk
125 g chicken liver pate

1 tablespoon sherry
1 teaspoon French
   mustard
1 tablespoon cream
salt and pepper
shredded lettuce, to serve

Form ham into cornets and secure with toothpick if necessary. Make white sauce by melting butter, stirring in flour and cooking 1 minute. Gradually add the milk and cook, stirring until thickened. Beat in pate, sherry and mustard. When smooth, stir in cream and season to taste.

Fill a piping bag fitting with a large plain nozzle and pipe mixture into each cornet. Remove toothpicks and serve on a bed of shredded lettuce.

Serves 4

COLD ROAST PORK

1.5 kg loin of pork,
   boned
1 tablespoon garlic salt
2 cloves garlic, sliced

1 tablespoon dried mixed
   herbs
3 tablespoons oil
1 cup claret

Remove rind from pork and sprinkle the meat with salt and leave to stand for about an hour.

Make several small slits in the meat and insert a slice of garlic into each. Sprinkle the inside of meat with salt and herbs, roll up and tie securely with string.

Brown meat in oil then pour over claret, cover with foil and bake at 190°C (375°F) for 1 hour 15 minutes, basting occasionally, until juice comes out clear when meat is pierced by a skewer. Serve cold, finely sliced.

Serves 6–8

JELLIED MEAT

Any leftover or delicatessen meats can be used. Add whichever stock is suitable and flavour with fresh herbs if desired.

4 cups chopped, cooked
   meat
½ cup chopped celery
1 egg, hard-boiled and
   chopped
½ cup chopped pickles

2 cups beef or chicken
   stock
salt and pepper
2 tablespoons gelatine
½ cup hot water

Mix chopped meat with celery, egg and pickles, stir in stock and season to taste. Dissolve gelatine in hot water and stir into mixture. Pour into a prepared mould and chill until set. Turn out on to a salad platter, and serve, finely sliced.

Serves 4

SAVOURY MOULD

Any kind of leftover cooked meat, poultry or continental sausage can be used in this recipe. For extra flavour, add herbs such as chopped mint with lamb or finely grated horseradish with beef. Instead of ham, try tongue or other sliced meat from the delicatessen.

1 cup chicken or beef
   stock
1 sachet (3 teaspoons)
   gelatine
1 hard-boiled egg, sliced
250 g cold meat, sliced or
   chopped

2 slices ham
2 tablespoons whipped
   cream, optional
Sauce Remoulade (see
   recipe)

Heat stock and dissolve gelatine. Arrange egg slices on the bottom of a prepared mould and barely cover with dissolved gelatine. Refrigerate until set.

Cover with meat and ham and pour over remaining gelatine. Chill until set and then turn out. Serve with Sauce Remoulade.

Serves 2–3
Note: 2 tablespoons whipped cream may be added to gelatine if desired.

Cornets de Jambon

Egg Dishes

Eggs occur unsung in a myriad of dishes such as crepes, fondues and blintzes but they deserve a fanfare on their own account. Ideally sized for entree dishes, their versatility and colouring offer a unique potential for both flavour and appearance.

Eggs can be served raw, cooked, hot, cold, whole or creamed, chopped and sliced. Delicious with very few accompaniments they are also a perfect complement to caviar, cheese, shellfish and spicy foods. They can form the basis of the most simple or most extravagant of courses.

Hens eggs are the most commonly used but, for that touch of individuality to a dish, quail or duck eggs may make an interesting alternative.

EGGS FLORENTINE

500 g spinach	*4 eggs*
20 g butter	*¾ cup grated cheese*

SAUCE

20 g butter	*½ cup milk*
1 tablespoon flour	

Cook spinach until just tender, drain and puree lightly. Toss in melted butter over low heat for a few minutes and then arrange in a shallow ovenproof dish or on 4 individual dishes. Melt butter, stir in flour and cook for 1 minute, gradually adding milk, stirring constantly and cooking until thickened and smooth.

Make holes in the centre of spinach to form a nest and break an egg into each. Sprinkle with cheese and spoon a little sauce over each egg. Bake at 180°C (360°F) for 15 minutes, until eggs are set and serve immediately.

Cheese and Prawn Souffles, Roquefort Crepes

Serves 4

EGGS BAKED ON WATERCRESS PUREE

1 large bunch watercress
90 g butter
1 large onion, finely
  chopped
2 cups chicken stock or
  water

salt and freshly ground
  black pepper
2 tablespoons flour
¾ cup milk
¼ cup cream
8 eggs

Pick the leaves off the watercress, wash well then shake off the excess water. Soften the chopped onion in 30 g butter, then stir in watercress and heat for 1–2 minutes. Pour in the stock (or water), bring to the boil, then reduce the heat and simmer, covered, for 15 minutes. Cool the mixture slightly then puree.

Simmer the puree in a pan until thick. Taste and season with salt and pepper, then spoon into 8 individual souffle dishes or ramekins.

Melt 60 g butter, add the flour and cook for 1–2 minutes. Remove from the heat and gradually add the milk, stirring constantly. Return to the heat and simmer until thickened. Stir the cream through and adjust the seasoning to taste.

Break 1 egg onto the watercress puree in each dish. Spoon an equal amount of sauce over the eggs, place the dishes in a water bath and bake at 180°C (350°F) until the eggs are set, about 10 minutes.

Serves 8

CHEESE AND PRAWN SOUFFLE

20 g butter
1 tablespoon flour
½ cup milk
1 cup grated mild cheese

6 eggs, separated
2 egg whites
125 g cooked prawns,
  peeled

Melt butter, stir in flour and cook for 1 minute, gradually adding the milk, stirring constantly, and cooking until thickened. Add cheese to sauce and cook over low heat, stirring constantly until cheese melts. Cool slightly then blend in egg yolks and prawns.

Whisk egg whites until stiff. Blend in half the egg whites with metal spoon, stirring well. Now lightly fold in the rest. Pour into 8 lightly greased individual souffle dishes and bake at 180°C (360°F) for 15 minutes. Serve immediately.

Serves 8
Note: Finely chopped leftover cold meat may be substituted for the prawns.

BLUE CHEESE AND PORT SOUFFLES

2 tablespoons Parmesan
  cheese
60 g butter
3 tablespoons flour
1½ cups milk
freshly ground pepper to
  taste

125 g good quality blue
  vein cheese
¼ cup port
¼ cup finely chopped
  pecans or walnuts
3 eggs, separated
1 extra egg white

Grease 6 individual souffle dishes, dusting them with the Parmesan cheese.

Heat the butter and add the flour, cooking for 2 minutes. Remove from the heat and add the milk gradually. Return to the heat and bring to the boil, then reduce the heat and simmer until thickened. Adjust the seasoning with pepper, according to taste.

Mash the blue vein cheese and combine with the port, mixing until smooth. Stir the cheese mixture and the nuts into the sauce with the egg yolks and beat well to combine all the ingredients. Taste and adjust the seasoning if necessary.

Whisk the egg whites until stiff. With a large metal spoon, fold ¼ of the whites into sauce then gradually add the remaining whites, cutting and folding in until they are incorporated.

Divide the mixture between 6 souffle dishes and bake in a water bath at 190°C (375°F) for 15–20 minutes, or until well risen and firm to the touch. Serve immediately.

Serves 6

CREPE BATTER

1½ cups flour
3 eggs
1¾ cups milk or half

milk, half stock
melted butter for cooking

Sift the flour into a bowl. Make a well in the centre and break in the eggs, stirring with a wooden spoon and gradually incorporating some of the flour. Pour in a little milk and, stirring from the centre, incorporate more of the flour. Keep adding the milk gradually, stirring to form a smooth batter. When all the liquid is added beat well. If the mixture is a little lumpy, either whisk or strain through a sieve. (Batter can also be prepared in a food processor or blender.)

Heat an 18 cm crepe pan, brush lightly with melted butter and pour in sufficient batter to just cover the base, tilting to coat evenly. Cook over a moderate heat until the surface is dry and the bottom golden. Turn and cook the other side. Repeat with the remaining batter, greasing the pan as necessary.

Makes approximately 16 crepes.

To keep crepes warm: As the crepes are cooked, stack on a heatproof plate, cover with foil and keep warm over a pan of simmering water.

To freeze crepes: Separate the crepes with a piece of greaseproof paper, place in a freezer bag in stacks of 6 or 8, and seal well, label and freeze — for up to 3 months.

Note: The side of the crepe that is cooked first always becomes the outside when rolled or folded. Generally, the first side has a more even colour while the second side has brown 'blisters'.

ROQUEFORT CREPES

16 Crepes (see recipe)
2 cups Bechamel Sauce (see recipe)
125 g Roquefort cheese or other good blue cheese
freshly grated nutmeg
salt and pepper
1 cup grated Cheddar cheese
cherry tomatoes and basil leaves, to garnish

Prepare the Bechamel Sauce. Mash the Roquefort cheese with a fork until smooth then gradually add to the sauce. Season with nutmeg, salt and pepper to taste. As Roquefort is fairly salty, watch the amount of salt added.

Spread 2 tablespoons of sauce on each crepe. Fold the crepe in half then into quarters. Arrange the crepes in an ovenproof dish, sprinkle with the cheese and bake at 200°C (400°F) until the cheese has melted.

When serving, arrange 2 crepes on each plate garnished with cherry tomatoes and basil leaves.

Serves 8

SEAFOOD AND SPINACH CREPES

2 cups Bechamel Sauce, made with 80g butter and 4 tablespoons flour (see recipe)
12 crepes (see recipe)
60 g butter
300 g scallops, cleaned
½ bunch shallots (spring onions, scallions), white part only, finely chopped
½ cup dry white wine
1 bunch English spinach or 250 g frozen spinach
250 g ricotta cheese, sieved
1 egg yolk
freshly ground pepper
freshly grated nutmeg
250 g smoked salmon
½ cup cream
½ cup natural yoghurt
lemon wedges
sprigs of fennel or flat-leaved parsley, to garnish

Prepare Bechamel Sauce and crepes and set aside.

Melt 20 g butter, add the scallops, cook for 2 minutes, then remove and slice. Cook 2 tablespoons of shallots in the pan until soft, then add the wine and simmer reducing the liquid to 2 tablespoons. Add the Bechamel Sauce and heat through, stirring in the scallops.

Wash the spinach well, shred the leaves and pack into a pan, cooking, covered, until tender. Drain the liquid.

Heat the remaining butter and add the remaining shallots, cooking until soft. Add the spinach and cook until the liquid has evaporated.

Combine the ricotta with egg yolk and spinach, seasoning with pepper and nutmeg to taste. Spread a portion over each crepe, top with smoked salmon then roll up and place in a greased ovenproof dish.

Scald the cream, combine with yoghurt and pour over the crepes. Bake at 190°C (375°F) until the crepes are heated through. Arrange 2 crepes on each plate, spoon over the heated scallop sauce and serve garnished with lemon wedges and sprigs of fennel or parsley.

Serves 6

Spinach: If fresh English spinach is unavailable, use a 250 g packet of frozen spinach and defrost following the instructions on the packet. If possible, avoid using silverbeet as the more pungent flavour may overpower the scallops and salmon.

Savoury Eclairs

CHEESE BLINTZES
CREPES

1 cup water
1 cup milk
2 cups flour
4 eggs
2 tablespoons oil

1 teaspoon sugar
½ teaspoon salt
oil for frying
butter for frying

FILLING

500 g ricotta cheese
250 g cream cheese
1 egg
1 tablespoon sugar

1 teaspoon vanilla
  essence
1 carton sour (dairy
  soured) cream, to serve

Blend the crepe ingredients thoroughly, allow to stand for 30 minutes, then stir to mix batter.

Lightly oil a crepe pan and heat over medium heat until a drop of water bounces when dropped on the surface. Pour 2 tablespoons of batter into the pan, tilting to spread the batter thinly over the pan. Cook crepe on one side only until set and tiny bubbles appear. Turn out onto a tea towel.

For the filling, blend cheeses together, then add egg, sugar and vanilla and mix well. Spoon a well-rounded tablespoon of filling onto the centre of the cooked side of the crepe. Fold up bottom edge, then each side and then top to form a rectangular parcel. Repeat until all the blintzes are made.

Fry blintzes in butter, seam side down, until browned, then turn and fry other side. Serve with sour cream.

Serves 6–8
Note: Blintzes may be prepared in advance to the second cooking stage then frozen. Arrange on a tray, without stacking, and freeze. When solid, pack in plastic bags, label and store in freezer. To serve, cook over low heat in butter in the frozen state.

66

SAVOURY ECLAIRS

1¼ cups water
120 g butter
1¼ cups flour, sifted
salt and freshly ground
    black pepper

¼ teaspoon paprika
4 eggs
lemon wedges
watercress

FILLING

60 g butter
3 tablespoons flour
1½ cups flavoured milk
    (see recipe)

300 g medium-sized
    cooked prawns, shells
    and veins removed
squeeze lemon juice

Bring water and 120 g butter to the boil until the butter melts. When the water boils, add the flour, salt and pepper to taste and the paprika. Remove from the heat, stir to blend, then return to the heat, cooking until the mixture comes away from the sides of the pan. Allow to cool for a few minutes.

Add the eggs, 1 at a time, beating well. Set oven temperature to 200°C (400°F) and sprinkle 2 baking trays with water.

Fill a piping bag fitted with a 1 cm plain nozzle with the pastry and pipe finger lengths of pastry onto the prepared trays, leaving sufficient space for spreading. (The mixture should make 16–18 eclairs). Bake for 20–25 minutes or until golden and cooked. Slit 1 side of the pastry and scrape out any uncooked dough.

Melt 60 g butter, stir in flour and add milk gradually, stirring constantly and cooking until thickened. Add the prawns and taste the sauce, adjust seasonings with salt, pepper and lemon juice.

Fill the eclairs with the hot prawn mixture. Arrange 2 eclairs on each plate and serve garnished with lemon wedges and watercress.

Serves 8

HONEY CHEESE CASSEROLE

500 g cream cheese
¾ cup sour cream

3 teaspoons honey
3 eggs, separated

Beat cheese and sour cream together until smooth, then mix in blended honey and egg yolks.

Beat egg whites until stiff and fold into the cheese mixture. Pour into greased, shallow, ovenproof dish and bake at 180°C (360°F) for 30 minutes. Serve hot.

Serves 4–6

CHEESE STRUDEL

250 g tasty cheese, grated
150 g mozzarella cheese,
    grated
100 g Parmesan cheese,
    grated
100 g mushrooms, sliced
2 tablespoons chopped
    parsley
2 teaspoons granulated
    garlic

½ teaspoon dried
    oregano
pinch cayenne
1 egg, beaten
4 sheets filo pastry
¼ cup melted butter
4 tablespoons dried
    breadcrumbs

Combine cheeses together in a large bowl and add mushrooms, parsley, garlic, oregano, cayenne and egg. Mix well and set aside.

Dampen a tea towel and lay on a flat surface, placing the first sheet of filo pastry on it and coating it with butter. Sprinkle with 2 tablespoons breadcrumbs and place the second pastry sheet over this and again coat with butter.

Take half the cheese mixture, compress, form a roll and place on the longer side of the pastry. Using the tea towel to lift the pastry sheets, roll up from cheese covered end, dabbing pastry with melted butter as you go.

Place on a baking sheet, seam side down and tuck in ends. Make the second roll the same way, then score each roll 6 times with a knife (to mark slices). Bake at 190°C (370°F) for 15-20 minutes until lightly browned. Cut through slices and serve.

Serves 6

CREAMY CURRIED EGGS

8 hard-boiled eggs
2 small onions, thinly
    sliced
175 g cream cheese
½ cup cream

2 teaspoons curry powder
freshly ground black
    pepper
paprika and parsley
    sprigs, to garnish

Slice eggs thinly, arrange in shallow serving dish and cover with onion slices. Blend remaining ingredients until well mixed and thick, then pour over the eggs. Garnish with sprinkling of paprika and parsley sprigs.

Serves 4–6

CAVIAR AND EGG PIE

8 hard-boiled eggs
125 g butter, melted
1 cup sour (dairy soured) cream
1 small onion, finely chopped
1 jar red caviar (lumpfish roe)
1 jar black caviar (lumpfish roe)
½ cup finely chopped parsley

Mash eggs with fork or blend for a few seconds. Combine well with butter and press into a 20 cm pie plate. Cover evenly with sour cream and sprinkle with chopped onion.

Decorate the pie with alternate segments of red caviar, black caviar and parsley, using a ruler or spatula as a guide. Delicious served with toast, savoury biscuits or salad.

Serves 6–8

STUFFED EGGS

12 eggs
⅔ cup mayonnaise, preferably home-made
1–2 teaspoons tomato paste
1 teaspoon chopped fresh basil leaves
1 tablespoon chopped fresh parsley
1 tablespoon snipped chives
1 teaspoon mustard
1 tablespoon curry paste
1 mignonette lettuce, washed and dried
watercress to garnish

Hard-boil the eggs, stirring gently for 2–3 minutes before they come to the boil — this helps to centre the yolks. Drain and cool the eggs in cold water, then shell them, cut in half lengthways and put the yolks in a bowl. Set the whites aside in another bowl and cover with water.

Mash the yolks with sufficient mayonnaise to bind them. Divide mixture into 3 equal portions. Flavour 1 portion with tomato paste and basil; 1 with herbs and mustard; and 1 with curry paste. Taste and adjust the seasoning and consistency of each flavour.

Drain the egg whites and pat dry them with absorbent paper. Place the tomato flavoured mixture into a piping bag fitted with a fluted nozzle and pipe into 8 whites. Repeat with the remaining 'flavours', piping each into 8 halves.

Arrange 2 mignonette leaves on each plate, top with 3 stuffed egg halves — 1 of each flavour and garnish with watercress.

Serves 8

CHICKEN MACARONI OMELETTE

250 g macaroni
60 g unsalted butter
1 cup Parmesan cheese
2 eggs
salt and pepper
2 tablespoons finely chopped parsley
2–3 tablespoons olive oil
2 cups cooked diced chicken

Boil macaroni in salted water for 10 minutes, drain and combine with butter and Parmesan cheese. Leave the mixture to cool, stirring occasionally to prevent sticking.

Whisk the eggs together with salt and pepper to taste and add 1 tablespoon parsley and the macaroni.

Heat olive oil in a frying pan and pour in omelette mix, cooking and turning to brown on both sides. When it is done, slice the omelette into 4 portions and place on serving plate.

Meanwhile heat the diced chicken through in the pan, scatter a little over each portion, garnish with parsley and serve.

Serves 4

CURRIED EGG LOG

375 g cream cheese
6 eggs, medium-boiled (6 minutes)
2 tablespoons melted butter
2 teaspoons curry powder
1–2 teaspoons lemon juice
1 loaf sliced wholemeal bread, crusts removed
parsley sprigs and sliced radishes, to garnish

Blend cheese, eggs, butter, curry powder and lemon juice to taste, checking flavour and adding more curry powder and/or lemon juice if desired.

Grease a loaf tin and arrange a layer of bread on the bottom, cutting to fit if necessary. Spread with a thin layer of cheese and egg mixture then cover with another layer of bread. Repeat layers, finishing with a layer of bread. Refrigerate for several hours, or overnight. To serve dip briefly into very hot water then turn log out onto serving plate. Garnish with parsley sprigs and sliced radishes

Serves 6–8

Note: Can be frozen in a non-metal container. To serve, remove from freezer, dip container briefly into very hot water, turn out onto serving plate and allow to thaw for about 2 hours.

Caviar and Egg Pie

EGG PILAU

1 cup long-grain rice
80 g butter
2 large onions, finely
   chopped
2 cloves garlic, crushed
2 tablespoons curry
   powder
½ cup raisins

½ cup sultanas
1 cinnamon stick or ¼
   teaspoon ground
   cinnamon
5 hard-boiled eggs,
   chopped
freshly ground black
   pepper

Cook rice and drain. Saute onion and garlic in butter until transparent. Add curry, raisins, sultanas and cinnamon stick (if using ground cinnamon, add this later with the eggs). Cover and simmer for 20 minutes over very low heat to allow flavours to develop.

Add chopped eggs and rice, season to taste and simmer for 10 minutes until heated through.

Serves 4

EGGPLANT FRY

1 large eggplant
   (aubergine)
2 eggs, lightly beaten
1½ cups dried
   breadcrumbs
oil for frying
6 eggs

¼ cup cream
2 tablespoons sherry
1 bottle oysters, drained
   and coarsely chopped
20 g butter
8 slices cheese

Slice eggplant into 8 slices each about 5 mm thick, dip in eggs and coat in breadcrumbs. Fry or grill until crisp and brown on both sides and arrange in a shallow ovenproof dish.

Beat eggs with cream and add sherry, oysters and butter. Cook over medium heat until butter is melted and the mixture thickens.

Spoon a mound of mixture on to the eggplant slices, cover each with cheese and cook under a hot grill until the cheese melts.

Serves 4

Note: A number of variations to this recipe are possible. Here are two suggestions.

• Add chives, crispy bacon or chopped ham to the basic mixture for variety.

• Instead of serving on eggplant, substitute muffins or thick toast rounds.

BLINI

30 g compressed yeast or
   2 sachets dried yeast
1½ cups lukewarm water
1 cup buckwheat flour
2 cups flour
3 eggs
salt and freshly ground
   pepper
120 g butter, melted

1 carton sour (dairy
   soured) cream
red and black lumpfish
   roe
smoked salmon
   (optional)
6 hard-boiled eggs,
   chopped

Stir the yeast gently into ½ cup of lukewarm water, then leave in a warm spot for a few minutes.

Sift the flours into a mixing bowl, make a well in the centre, add the yeast mixture, 1 cup of lukewarm water, the eggs, salt and pepper and 2 tablespoons of the melted butter. With clean hands, mix all the ingredients from the centre gradually incorporating the flour. Now beat the mixture until smooth. Cover and leave in a warm place to double.

Stir the batter well then leave for another 30 minutes, before stirring again.

Heat a heavy-based frying pan and brush with a little of the melted butter. Pour in ¼ cup of the batter and cook until the underside is golden and the top surface dry, then turn and cook the other side. Keep warm while making the remaining blini.

Arrange the blini on a serving plate and serve with the remaining melted butter, sour cream, lumpfish roe, smoked salmon and eggs.

Serves 8

Blini

Sauces

Sauces enhance the flavours of meat and sea-food dishes and can liven up even the plainest steak. The most basic white sauce is open to many variations and with a little imagination cheeses and herbs can alter its flavour and texture.

Sauces are meant to complement a dish, to add that final touch and not dominate the dish. So don't use too much. Its often a good idea to put the sauce in a separate dish on the table and then it's not your responsibility if someone chooses to use a lot of sauce.

If the sauce is not being used immediately, cut a circle of greaseproof paper the same diameter as the saucepan used to prepare the sauce, and lay the circle over the sauce so that the paper touches the sauce. This will prevent a skin forming.

BASIC WHITE SAUCE

This very simple sauce has a myriad of uses. For variety, add cheese or fresh herbs or replace the milk with stock. In cooking, add the liquid gradually to the roux (the butter and flour combination) and stir the sauce constantly to avoid lumps.

30 g butter
1 tablespoon flour
1 cup milk

Melt the butter in a medium-sized saucepan and when it starts to foam, add the flour, stirring vigorously with a wooden spoon over a low heat for 1 minute. Remove the saucepan from the heat and add the milk a little at a time, stirring constantly.

If the sauce begins turning lumpy stop adding the milk and beat hard until the lumps have dissolved. Continue to add the milk until all has been used.

Return to the heat and stir until thickened and the sauce starts to boil. Boil for 3 minutes then serve.

Makes 1 cup

MORNAY SAUCE

1 cup Basic White Sauce (see recipe)
1 egg, beaten

3 tablespoons grated cheese

Blend 1 tablespoon of the hot Basic White Sauce into the egg yolk and beat with a wooden spoon. Mix into remaining sauce with the cheese and re-heat, stirring until smooth. Do not allow to boil.

Makes 1 cup

CHEESE SAUCE

1 cup Basic White Sauce (see recipe)
⅓ cup grated tasty cheddar cheese

1 tablespoon Parmesan cheese (optional)
pinch nutmeg

Combine all ingredients in a saucepan with the Basic White Sauce and stir constantly over a low heat until the cheese melts and the sauce is heated through. Serve with vegetables or cured meat dishes.

Makes 1 cup

BECHAMEL SAUCE

A true French sauce enhanced with the flavours of onion, bay leaves, cloves and celery

1¾ cups milk
1 small onion, peeled
2 cloves
2 bay leaves
few celery leaves

6 peppercorns
100 g butter
⅓ cup flour
¼ cup cream

Place the milk in a heavy-based saucepan and add the onion, studded with cloves, the bay leaves, celery and peppercorns. Bring to the boil then cover and remove from the heat. Allow to cool then strain and discard the flavourings.

Melt the butter and when it starts to foam, add the flour and heat, stirring constantly for 2–3 minutes before removing from the heat and gradually add the milk. Return to the heat and bring to the boil, stirring constantly. Cook a further 3 minutes then reduce the heat and simmer until the mixture is smooth and thick. Stir in the cream.

Makes 2 cups

COURT BOUILLON

1 litre water
1 teaspoon salt
1 small carrot, sliced
1 bay leaf
3 parsley stalks

¼ cup white wine or vinegar
60 g onion sliced
sprig thyme

Combine all ingredients in a large saucepan and bring slowly to the boil. Reduce the heat and simmer covered for 30 minutes. Strain before using.

Makes 1 litre

Mussels en Brochette with Easy Bearnaise Sauce

Deep-fried Crepes with Veal and Mushrooms served with Tomato Sauce

SAUCE VELOUTE

60 g butter
½ cup flour

2⅓ cups rich chicken stock

Melt the butter in a saucepan and when it starts to foam add the flour and stir over a medium heat until the mixture has a sandy texture. Remove from heat and gradually add the hot stock, stirring constantly until smooth.

Return to the heat and stir until thickened. Allow to boil then reduce the heat and simmer for 10–15 minutes.

Makes about 2½ cups
Sauce Veloute can be made in a number of different ways — here are a couple of ideas for inspiration: Sauce Supreme and Sauce Aurora.

SAUCE SUPREME

2 cups Veloute Sauce
1 egg yolk

3 tablespoons cream
2 tablespoons lemon juice

Prepare the Veloute Sauce and keep warm. Beat the egg yolk with the cream and blend in 2 tablespoons Veloute Sauce, stirring constantly to mix well. Add the remaining sauce and stir, adding the lemon juice gradually.

Makes about 2¾ cups

SAUCE AURORA

1 tablespoon tomato
puree

2¾ cups Sauce Supreme

Prepare the Sauce Supreme and then add the tomato puree, mixing well until the sauce becomes slightly pink.

Makes about 2¾ cups

WHITE WINE SAUCE

90 g butter
3 tablespoons flour
1 cup fish stock
2 tablespoons dry white
wine

2 tablespoons cream
salt and cayenne pepper
few drops lemon juice

Melt 30 g butter in small saucepan and add flour, stirring with a wooden spoon over low heat for 1–2 minutes. When the mixture becomes a light fawn colour add stock gradually and stir until boiling. Simmer for 10 minutes, whisk in wine and remove from heat. Gradually beat in remaining butter and stir in cream. Add seasonings and lemon juice to taste. Before serving, strain sauce through a fine sieve.

Makes 1 cup

SABAYON SAUCE

3 egg yolks
juice ½ lemon
¼ teaspoon salt

cayenne pepper
½ cup cream
¼ cup dry white wine

Combine all ingredients in the top half of a double boiler or in a heatproof bowl placed over a saucepan of simmering water. Whisk constantly over the water until the sauce thickens to a creamy consistency. One test for when the sauce is ready is if it clings to the whisk when it is lifted from sauce. Serve immediately over fresh asparagus or other fresh vegetables.

Makes approximately 1½ cups

HOLLANDAISE SAUCE

3 tablespoons white wine
vinegar
5 black peppercorns
1 shallot (spring onion,
scallion), chopped
½ bay leaf
3 egg yolks

180–250 g unsalted
butter, cut into cubes
and slightly softened
salt and white pepper to
taste
squeeze lemon juice
fresh dill, to garnish

Simmer vinegar, peppercorns, shallot and bay leaf together in a small saucepan until the mixture reduces to 3 teaspoons. Strain and set aside.

Place the egg yolks and 1 tablespoon of butter together in a heatproof bowl and whisk together, adding the flavoured vinegar. Place the bowl over a saucepan of gently simmering water making sure that the bowl does not touch the water.

Whisk the sauce constantly adding the butter a little at a time. If the butter is added too quickly, the sauce may curdle. You may not need all the butter but the finished sauce should be a light, creamy colour, foamy consistency and thick enough to coat the back of a metal spoon. Use immediately over meat or seafood dishes.

Makes 1½–2 cups

EASY BEARNAISE SAUCE

1 cup Basic White Sauce (see recipe)	*white of shallot (spring onion, scallion)*
2 tablespoons wine vinegar	*pinch salt*
2 tablespoons dry white wine	*pinch white pepper*
1 teaspoon dried tarragon	*2 egg yolks, lightly beaten*
2 teaspoons chopped	*2 tablespoons soft butter*

Prepare Basic White Sauce then set it aside with a covering of greaseproof paper.

Simmer vinegar and wine with herbs, shallot and seasonings until the liquid is reduced by half, then strain. Pour White Sauce over egg yolks, whisk, then add butter and the reduced liquid. Beat thoroughly and serve immediately.

Makes 1½ cups

GREEN BEAN PUREE

1 cup chicken consomme (canned)	*¼ cup toasted slivered almonds*
90 g butter	*finely ground black pepper*
500 g French beans	
½ cup sour (dairy soured) cream	

Combine the consomme and butter in a pan, bring to the boil. Then add the beans and cook until tender. Drain, reserving the liquid.

Refresh the beans in cold water and then puree in a food processor or blender, adding the reserved liquid.

Deep-fried Cheese Scallops with Chilli Tomato Sauce

Return to pan and simmer over low heat, stirring in sour cream and heating until almost boiling. Add the slivered almonds and pepper.

Makes approximately 3 cups

TOMATO COULIS

This lightly seasoned sauce adds colour and interest and can be used to cover the base of a plate with the food placed on top. This is most effective if the serving plate is of a contrasting colour.

750 g tomatoes, cored, peeled and seeded	*pinch sugar*
40 g butter	*salt and pepper to taste*
3 shallots (spring onions, scallions), finely chopped	*small bouquet garni*

Place the tomatoes in a food processor or blender and process until pureed.

Melt the butter in a medium-sized saucepan adding the shallots and cooking for 2–3 minutes until softened. Mix in the remaining ingredients and add to the tomatoes. Cover and cook over a low heat for 20 minutes or until it has thickened.

Makes approximately 3 cups

75

FRESH TOMATO SAUCE

500 g tomatoes, cored
  and peeled
30 g butter
salt and pepper
pinch sugar

½ teaspoon fresh basil,
  chopped
1 tablespoon tomato
  paste

Chop tomatoes roughly and bring to the boil with butter, salt, pepper, sugar, basil and tomato paste. Reduce the heat and simmer uncovered for 20 minutes. Strain sauce and set aside. The sauce will keep refrigerated for 10 days.

Makes 4 cups

QUICK TOMATO SAUCE

1 onion, chopped
2 cloves garlic, chopped
1 tablespoon fresh basil,
  chopped
1 tablespoon olive oil

425 g can tomatoes,
  roughly chopped
salt and pepper
1 teaspoon sugar

Saute onion, garlic and basil in oil for 3 minutes, then add tomato pieces, salt, pepper and sugar and top up with liquid. Bring to the boil and simmer for 20 minutes, then puree in blender or food processor. Adjust seasonings to taste.

Makes approximately 2 cups

CHILLI TOMATO SAUCE

1 tablespoon oil
½ medium onion,
  chopped
1 clove garlic, finely
  chopped
1 large tomato peeled,
  deseeded and chopped

pinch basil and sugar
salt and freshly ground
  pepper
1 tablespoon tomato
  paste
1 teaspoon chilli sauce

Heat the oil in a medium-sized saucepan and add the onion and garlic. Cook until the onion becomes transparent.

Add tomato, seasonings and tomato paste and cook gently for 15–20 minutes, adding a little water (or stock) if mixture becomes too dry. Blend in chilli sauce. If you like your sauces sharp — add an extra teaspoon of chilli sauce. Spoon mixture into an electric blender or processor and puree before serving.

Makes approximately 1 cup

CURRY SAUCE

15 g butter
1 onion, chopped
1 small clove garlic,
  crushed
3 teaspoons flour
1½ teaspoons curry
  powder
2 teaspoons tomato puree
1¼ cups fish stock or
  coconut milk

½ apple, peeled and
  chopped
1 tablespoon fruit
  chutney
2 teaspoons coconut
2 tablespoons natural
  yoghurt or cream

Melt the butter in saucepan and lightly cook the onions and garlic until the onion becomes transparent. Stir in flour and curry powder and gently heat until a sandy colour. Gradually stir in the tomato puree and stock and stir until smooth and boiling. Add remaining ingredients and season to taste. Reduce heat and allow to simmer for 15 minutes before serving hot with natural yoghurt or cream folded through.

Makes 2 cups

Plaited Sole Fillets with Tartare Sauce

Shellfish Cocktail served with Cocktail Sauce

MAYONNAISE

A very popular cold sauce with many exciting variations, two classics being Green Sauce and Tartare Sauce. Mayonnaise blends particularly well with the flavours of chicken, seafood and eggs.

4 egg yolks
salt and freshly ground
* pepper*
1 teaspoon prepared

mustard
1 cup vegetable oil
1-2 tablespoons white
* wine vinegar*

Whisk egg yolks, salt, pepper and mustard together until thick, then gradually add the oil, drop by drop whisking constantly until ¼ cup has been incorporated. Add the rest of the oil in a thin steady stream and continue to whisk. Check the consistency occasionally and when the mayonnaise begins to thicken and whisking is difficult, add a little vinegar to thin down the sauce.

When all the oil is incorporated, taste and adjust the seasoning with salt, pepper and vinegar.
Makes 1 cup
To store: Mayonnaise will keep in the refrigerator for about 10 days. To prevent a 'skin' forming on the mayonnaise, put a piece of plastic directly onto the surface of the mayonnaise.
Variations: Freshly chopped herbs of your choice can be added to the mayonnaise. Tomato paste or granules; curry paste; capers; chopped gherkins or different flavoured vinegar can also be used to give the mayonnaise a different flavour.

GREEN SAUCE

60 g spinach leaf, rinsed
* and chopped*
2 teaspoons chopped
* fresh tarragon*
2 teaspoons chopped
* fresh chervil*

2 tablespoons chopped
* fresh chives or*
* watercress*
1 cup mayonnaise

Blanch the spinach and herbs then refresh in cold water. Squeeze dry with a clean tea towel before adding to the Mayonnaise and blending well. Serve over pasta or seafood or as a dipping sauce for prawns.

Makes 2½ cups

TARTARE SAUCE

1 cup mayonnaise
60 g gherkin, finely diced

30 g capers, chopped
parsley, finely chopped

Combine all the ingredients in a bowl and mix together until smooth consistency. Tartare Sauce can be served as an accompaniment to most seafood dishes whether hot or cold.

Store in a well-sealed jar, preferably glass, in the refrigerator for up to 10 days if home-made Mayonnaise was used, or for about one month otherwise.

Makes 1 cup

SEAFOOD SAUCE

This sauce is delicious served with oysters or other cold seafood dishes

300 mL cream, lightly
* whipped*
½ cup tomato sauce

salt and pepper
few drops strained lemon
* juice*

Gently fold all the ingredients for the sauce together and chill before serving.

Makes 2 cups

COCKTAIL SAUCE

1 egg yolk
pinch salt, white pepper
* and English mustard*
2 teaspoons white vinegar

5 tablespoons olive oil
3 tablespoons tomato
* juice*

Place yolk, seasonings and vinegar in a bowl and whisk until light in colour. Gradually pour into the oil drop by drop at first and then when most of the oil has been added pour the oil in a little faster. Taste the sauce and correct the seasonings. Stir in the tomato juice and serve with fresh seafood.

Makes ¾ cup

Mustard Sauce with Pesto-stuffed Veal

FRESH HERB SAUCE

4 hard-boiled, shelled
  eggs
¼ cup thickened cream
  (double cream)
⅓ cup olive or peanut oil
1 tablespoon tarragon
  vinegar

½ bunch chives, washed
  and snipped
2 tablespoons chopped
  dill
2 tablespoons chopped
  parsley

Halve the eggs, remove yolks and finely chop the
whites. Push the yolks through a sieve and combine
with the cream, whisking until smooth and thick.
Gradually whisk the oil into this and add the vinegar
and herbs. Taste and adjust the seasoning with salt
and pepper.

Makes 1 cup

PIQUANT SAUCE

4 anchovy fillets
2 tablespoons capers
6 shallots (spring onions,
  scallions), chopped
2 cloves garlic, roughly
  chopped
1 teaspoon fresh basil or
  ¼ teaspoon dried

2 tablespoons olive oil
1 tablespoon finely
  chopped parsley
juice of ½ lemon
salt and pepper to taste

Puree anchovies, capers, shallots, garlic and basil in
food processor or blender. Add oil, parsley and lemon
juice and season to taste.
    Serve with a tomato salad or tossed through steam-
ing hot pasta.

Makes approximately ¾ cup

YOGHURT SAUCE

1 tablespoon chopped
  parsley
1 small clove garlic,
  crushed

1 cup natural yoghurt
few drops sesame oil
2 teaspoons chopped
  fresh chives

Combine all the ingredients in a glass bowl. Refrigerate well before serving with salad or as a dipping
sauce for a selection of fresh vegetables cut into straw
lengths.

Makes 1¼ cups

GLOUCESTER SAUCE

2 cups very thick
  mayonnaise
½ cup sour (dairy
  soured) cream
juice 1 lemon

1 teaspoon chopped fresh
  fennel
1 teaspoon
  Worcestershire sauce

Gradually add sour cream and lemon juice to mayonnaise, stirring until smooth. Flavour with fennel and
sauce according to taste. Serve with cold sliced
poultry.

Makes 2½ cups

SAUCE REMOULADE

1 cup mayonnaise
1 teaspoon French
  mustard
1 teaspoon English
  mustard
1 teaspoon chopped
  capers

1 teaspoon chopped
  gherkins
1 teaspoon chopped
  mixed herbs (parsley,
  tarragon and chervil)
2 anchovy fillets,
  chopped

Simply mix all the above ingredients together until
thoroughly blended. This sauce is a perfect
accompaniment to the Savoury Jellied Meat Mould
(see recipe) and other cold meats.

Makes 1 cup

MUSTARD SAUCE

20 g butter
2½ tablespoons dry
    mustard
1 tablespoon brown sugar
1 teaspoon salt
freshly ground black
    pepper

2 eggs, beaten
2 tablespoons water
¼ cup white wine
300 mL sour (dairy
    soured) cream

Melt butter over low heat and add mustard, sugar, seasonings and eggs. Stir over low heat for a few minutes, gradually adding water and wine until sauce thickens. Do not allow to boil. Allow to cool and then stir in sour cream.

Makes 1½ cups

Cold Curried Sauce with Arabian Meat Loaf

CUMBERLAND SAUCE

1 orange
1 lemon
½ cup port
3 tablespoons red-currant
    jelly
1 teaspoon mustard

pinch cayenne pepper
pinch ground ginger
1 teaspoon arrowroot
    combined with 2
    teaspoons water

Peel orange and lemon and cut rind into very fine strips — enough to fill 1 teaspoon of each. Blanch the strips by plunging them into boiling water for a few seconds and then drain.

Mix strips with remaining ingredients over heat, stirring constantly until jelly has dissolved. Thicken with arrowroot and water mixture if desired and add to sauce while it is boiling.

Refrigerate the sauce a day or two before serving with cold meats.

Makes ⅔ cup

COLD CURRIED SAUCE

For something different, serve this Cold Curried Sauce with your favourite cooked meat or sausage.

⅓ cup mayonnaise
⅔ cup yoghurt
lemon juice, to taste

curry paste or powder, to
    taste

Mix all the ingredients together and taste. Adjust the seasonings and if you prefer a sharp flavour add extra curry paste.

This sauce can be made into larger quantities using the above proportions and it is delicious over cooked meats or sausages.

Makes 1 cup

ANCHOVY AND CAPER SAUCE

2 tablespoons capers,
    finely chopped
4 anchovy fillets, finely
    chopped

2 tablespoons olive oil

Mix the capers and anchovies and heat in oil without boiling. Cool and serve with cold tongue or continental sausages.

Makes ¼ cup

79

Vegetables and Salads

Vegetables are perhaps the most versatile of all ingredients for appetisers. Some are bland; others have a quite distinctive flavour. On their own, vegetables are generally light and delicate, and are eminently suited to pastry dishes, souffles, or used in a creamy mousse. A vegetable alters its character quite radically according to the recipe — just compare stuffed zucchini to the souffled version.

The range of colour and texture of vegetables gives you the opportunity for experimenting — a terrine of vegetables in different hues can make a dramatically elegant impact, while there are endless possibilities with swirled and shaped purees and coulis, colourful roulades, dainty juliennes, or just a selection of roughly chopped and tossed salad ingredients.

The virtue of most vegetables is that they are seldom too filling, so even when prepared with cream, pastry or cheese, a starter-sized offering will never be overwhelming.

PUMPKIN TRIANGLES

750 g pumpkin, peeled, seeded and chopped
1 large onion, chopped
1 clove garlic, crushed
120 g butter
salt and pepper, to taste
¼ teaspoon cinnamon
⅔ cup Parmesan cheese
½ cup fresh breadcrumbs
½ cup sour (dairy soured) cream
2 egg yolks
½ cup oil
1 packet filo pastry

Cool the pumpkin until tender and mash it well. Gently saute the onion and garlic in 60 g butter until soft then combine with the pumpkin. Season with salt and pepper and add the cinnamon, ⅓ cup Parmesan cheese, breadcrumbs, sour cream and egg yolks and set aside to cool.

Melt the remaining butter, combine with the oil and liberally brush over 2 sheets of filo pastry. Place the pastry sheets 1 on top of the other and cut into 8 cm wide strips. Keep the other sheets of filo pastry covered with a damp cloth.

Place 2 teaspoons of filling in the bottom left corner of each strip and fold over to form a triangle. Continue 'somersaulting' the triangle to the end of the strip then place, seam down, on the baking tray. Follow this procedure for the remaining filling and pastry. Sprinkle the triangles with Parmesan cheese and bake at 190°C (375°F) for about 15 minutes or until golden.

Makes about 30 triangles

Pumpkin Filo Triangles

ARTICHOKE HEARTS STUFFED WITH CAMEMBERT

8 canned artichoke
    hearts, chokes
    removed
150 g Camembert
120 g asparagus,
    trimmed, peeled and
    cut into 2.5 cm
1 cup cream

¼ cup chopped shallots
    (spring onions,
    scallions)
60 g butter
1 large tomato, peeled,
    seeded and chopped
2 teaspoons chopped
    fresh dill

Arrange artichoke hearts in an ovenproof dish. Cut Camembert into small cubes and carefully fill hearts. Cover with foil and warm in oven. Quickly cook asparagus in boiling salted water until tender, then drain and refresh. Puree with 2 tablespoons cream. Saute shallots in butter then add asparagus puree, tomato, dill and rest of the cream. Reduce the sauce gradually until thickened, then season to taste and spoon over the artichoke hearts and serve.

Serves 4

ASPARAGUS SABAYON

1 kg fresh asparagus
1 large carrot

1 cup Sabayon Sauce (see
    recipe)

Lie the asparagus flat in a pan and cook in boiling, salted water until crispy tender. Drain and refresh in ice-cold water and set aside.

Peel the carrot, wash and dry it. With a vegetable peeler, peel 4 long strips from the carrot. Steam these until soft then use them to tie together 4 bundles of asparagus spears.

Serve each bundle on a plate with a dollop of Sabayon Sauce on the side.

Serves 4

SPINACH CREAM MOULD

1 kg English spinach,
    washed
sprig rosemary
40 g butter
8 tablespoons fine white
    breadcrumbs, soaked
    in ½ cup hot milk or
    cream

1 egg
1 extra egg yolk
salt and pepper
nutmeg
browned crumbs
grilled bacon cubes and
    sauteed mushrooms,
    for garnishing

Gently sweat spinach with a sprig of rosemary in a covered pan until it is tender. Drain on absorbent paper then puree. Return to saucepan with butter, and heat to reduce moisture. Allow to cool then add crumbs and beaten eggs and season well.

Fill 4 buttered, crumbed individual moulds and cover with buttered paper. Stand in a water bath and bake at 180°C (360°F) for 20 minutes until mould is firm to touch. Stand for 2–3 minutes before unmoulding and garnishing with bacon on mushroom caps. Serve hot with Yoghurt or Cheese Sauce (see recipes).

Serves 4

SPINACH ROULADE

400 g spinach, stalks
    removed
15 g butter
salt and pepper
pinch nutmeg

4 eggs separated
2 tablespoons grated
    Parmesan cheese
watercress and cherry
    tomatoes, to garnish

FILLING

180 g mushrooms, thinly
    sliced
15 g butter
1 tablespoon flour

salt and pepper to taste
½ cup milk
nutmeg

Prepare the filling first. Saute mushrooms in butter, add the flour and seasonings then pour in the milk, stirring until boiling. Reduce heat and simmer until the filling is creamy then add nutmeg to flavour.

Set oven at 220°C (425°F). Prepare a Swiss roll tin by lining it with greased greaseproof paper.

Steam spinach until softened and tender. Puree then stir in the butter, season and add egg yolks. Whip egg whites stiffly and fold into the mixture, cutting them in carefully with a spoon. Pile mixture into prepared tin and spread mixture quickly to 1.5 cm thickness. Sprinkle with Parmesan cheese and bake in oven 10–12 minutes until firm and puffed.

When cooked, turn the roulade onto a sheet of greaseproof paper. Remove cooking paper carefully and spread over the filling and roll up.

Slice the roulade diagonally and garnish portions with watercress and cherry tomatoes.

Serves 4–6

CAULIFLOWER AND OYSTER GRATIN

4 large cauliflower florets	squeeze of lemon juice
40 g butter	and a little grated zest
2 tablespoons flour	16 oysters
1½ cups milk	grated cheese
½ teaspoon grated onion	white breadcrumbs
salt and pepper	parsley for garnishing

Cook and drain the cauliflower florets and keep warm. Melt the butter, add flour and cook 3 minutes stirring in the milk until boiling. Season with grated onion, salt, pepper, lemon juice and zest. Add the oysters.

Place cauliflower florets in 4 individual serving bowls. Spoon over sauce and top with grated cheese and breadcrumbs. Heat through in oven to melt cheese. Sprinkle with parsley and serve.

Serves 4

ZUCCHINI SOUFFLE

500 g zucchini	1 cup cream
(courgettes), sliced	salt and pepper
3 red chillies, seeded,	pinch chilli powder or
toasted and cut into	cayenne
thin rings	2 fresh tomatoes sliced
1½ cups grated cheese	1 cup Cucumber Sauce
4 eggs	(see recipe)

Cook zucchini in boiling salted water for 2–3 minutes. Refresh in cold water and drain well. Arrange on a large round oven-to-table platter. Sprinkle with chilli rings and ½ the cheese.

Beat the eggs lightly, add the cream, salt, pepper and chilli. Pour over zucchini. Layer the tomato slices on the top, sprinkle over the remaining cheese and bake at 220°C (425°F) for 10–15 minutes, until puffed and brown.

Cut into wedges and serve with Cucumber Sauce.

Serves 4

ZUCCHINI RIPIENE

6 medium-sized zucchini	1¼ cups fresh grated
(courgettes)	Parmesan cheese
2 eggs	salt and pepper, to taste
¼ cup white	oregano
breadcrumbs	

Cook zucchini in boiling salted water for 6 minutes until just tender. Refresh in cold water then drain and dry. Cut in half, lengthways, scoop out pulp, leaving firm shell walls. Reserve the pulp. Drain shells upside down on kitchen paper. Puree zucchini pulp with eggs and breadcrumbs and Parmesan then season to taste.

Arrange the shells in greased gratin dish and pipe in the filling. Bake at 210°C (420°F) for 15–20 minutes or until filling is puffed and brown.

Serves 6

NUT-TOPPED ZUCCHINI

6 medium-sized zucchini	1 onion diced
(courgettes)	1 tablespoon vinegar
½ cauliflower separated	salt and pepper to taste
into florets	½ teaspoon cinnamon
2 tablespoons oil	1 tablespoon finely
1 red capsicum (pepper),	chopped parsley
diced	

NUT TOPPING

½ cup blanched chopped	1 tablespoon sugar
toasted almonds	1 tablespoon vinegar
½ cup dried	pinch salt
breadcrumbs	

Blanch zucchini in boiling salted water, refresh then drain. Cut in half, lengthways, and remove centres keeping wall intact. Cook cauliflower florets until tender, refresh then drain them and cut into small pieces.

Heat oil in saucepan, add capsicum and onion and cook until golden. Add the cauliflower and heat through then stir in the vinegar salt, pepper and cinnamon.

Pile filling into zucchini cases. Combine the ingredients for nut topping and spoon over surface. Arrange in an ovenproof dish and heat through in the oven at 180°C (360°F). Serve sprinkled with chopped parsley.

Serves 6

PASTRY SHELLS FOR VEGETABLES

PATE BRISEE

125 g butter, cubed
1 egg yolk
pinch salt

2 cups flour, sifted
¼ cup water

Blend butter, egg yolk and salt together in processor, then add flour and water and process until mixture just combines. Remove and knead into a ball but do not handle too much. Wrap in plastic film and rest in refrigerator for 1 hour.

Cut greaseproof paper to fit individual flan tins and grease lightly.

Roll out pastry on a floured surface, cut circles and line flan tins. Roll off edge with rolling pin. Chill flan tins in refrigerator.

Place greaseproof paper (greased side to pastry) in tins, weight with beans and bake blind for 5 minutes at 230°C (450°F).

Remove paper and beans, lower temperature to 180°C (360°F) and cook another 10 minutes, until golden. Cool slightly then unmould. Pastry shells can be stored in airtight tin until they are needed.

Makes 8

RATATOUILLE TARTLETS

1 onion, sliced in rings
2 tablespoons olive oil
2 cloves garlic, crushed
2 zucchini (courgettes),
    cut into slices
1 capsicum (pepper),
    seeded
400 g can tomatoes
1 small eggplant
    (aubergine), diced

bouquet garni of 3
    marjoram sprigs, 2
    thyme sprigs, 1 parsley
    sprig, ½ bay leaf
salt and freshly ground
    black pepper
6 Pastry Shells (see
    recipe)

Saute onion in oil, add garlic and cook for 1 minute. Add zucchini, capsicum, tomatoes, eggplant, bouquet garni and seasoning. Cover and simmer for 15 minutes. When cool, fill the pastry shells and serve.

Serves 6

RATATOUILLE WITH CHOKOES

2 onions, sliced
2 cloves garlic, crushed
2 tablespoons oil
4 chokoes peeled,
    quartered and cored
2 small eggplants
    (aubergines), cubed
4 zucchini (courgettes),
    sliced thickly
2 green capsicums
    (peppers), seeded and
    diced

3 sticks celery, prepared
    and sliced on diagonal
500 g tomatoes, peeled,
    seeded and quartered
1 teaspoon basil
salt and freshly ground
    black pepper

Saute onions and garlic in oil to soften. Add chokoes, eggplant, zucchini, capsicum and celery and cook for 5 minutes then add the tomatoes. Season, cover and simmer, stirring occasionally. Remove lid and reduce liquid slightly. Vegetables should retain their shape and texture.

For a puree, the mixture is cooked for a longer period.

Serves 4–6

ONION TART

Shortcrust pastry base

FILLING

2 onions, sliced thinly
1 tablespoon oil
½ teaspoon paprika
120 g Gruyere cheese,
    grated
120 g Emmenthal cheese,
    grated

2 eggs
1 cup cream, or ½ cup
    milk and ½ cup cream
salt
nutmeg

Saute onions gently in oil until soft, then stir in paprika. Mix ½ cheese with onions and scatter over the pastry base. Spread the rest of the cheese on top.

Beat the eggs and cream together and season with salt and nutmeg. Spoon over the cheese and bake at 180°C (360°F) for 25 minutes. Increase heat to 200°C (400°F) for the last 5 minutes of cooking time so that the top will puff and brown.

Serves 4

Ratatouille Tartlet

EGGPLANT GALETTE

5 eggplants (aubergines)
clove garlic, crushed
1 medium-sized onion,
  finely chopped
⅔ cup olive oil
500 g tomatoes, skinned,
  seeded and chopped

1 tablespoon tomato
  paste
1 teaspoon sugar
salt and pepper
200 g natural yoghurt
¼ cup stock

Slice eggplant thinly, sprinkle with salt and allow to stand. Saute garlic and onion in 2 tablespoons of oil for 4 minutes. Add tomatoes, mixing in tomato paste, sugar, salt and pepper and set aside.

Wipe the eggplant slices, brush with oil and grill them under a medium heat, regularly turning and brushing with oil until they are golden. Arrange a layer of eggplant on bottom and around the sides of an ovenproof dish. Spread the tomato pulp and yoghurt on top then continue to layer the ingredients, finishing with eggplant. Reserve ⅓ of the tomato pulp to make a sauce.

Cover with foil and press down lightly and bake at 180°C (360°F) for 30–40 minutes. Stand for few minutes before turning out onto a serving plate.

Combine the pulp and stock, reduce, pour over galette, sprinkle with chopped parsley and serve hot.

Serves 6

RED CABBAGE AND APPLE

20 g butter
1 medium-sized red
  cabbage, finely
  shredded
2 tablespoons honey

½ grated onion
1 grated apple
2 tablespoons lemon juice
¼ cup red wine

Melt the butter in large pan and saute the finely shredded cabbage with the honey. Add the onion, apple, lemon juice and wine, bring to the boil and simmer, covered, for 1 hour, shaking pan occasionally during cooking.

Serves 6–8

VEGETABLE STRUDEL

2 shallots (spring onions,
  scallions), finely
  chopped
150 g mushrooms, sliced
  thinly
60 g butter
1 tomato, peeled, seeded
  and cut into strips
1 white turnip, peeled
1 carrot, peeled
1 stalk celery
1 small fennel bulb
1 red capsicum (pepper)
1 cucumber, peeled

1 zucchini (courgette)
4 French beans, cut into
  thin diagonal slices
1 teaspoon mixed herbs,
  parsley, tarragon,
  chervil
lemon juice
salt and pepper to taste
6 sheets of filo pastry
oil or melted butter for
  brushing

Saute shallots and mushrooms in butter, add tomato and cook for 5 minutes then set aside. Prepare vegetables, cut them into matchstick-length strips, then cook 5 minutes in boiling salted water. Refresh in cold water, drain and toss with sauteed mixture, adding herbs, lemon juice, salt and pepper to taste. Brush filo sheets with oil and stack 1 on top of the other.

Place the vegetables on the pastry and roll up tucking in the ends. Brush with oil or melted butter and make 3–4 fine diagonal slits on top of pastry. Bake at 200°C (400°F) until pastry is flaked and golden, about 25–30 minutes.

Serve cut into diagonal slices with Green Bean Puree (see recipe) or Tomato Coulis (see recipe).

Serves 4–6

HOT CURRIED SLAW

½ large cabbage,
  shredded
1 bay leaf
2 garlic cloves
1 cup stock
salt and pepper
1 onion spiked with 2
  cloves

1½ tablespoons flour
1 tablespoon curry
  powder
40 g butter
¾ cup cream
¼ cup buttered
  breadcrumbs

Combine bay leaf, garlic and cabbage in a large saucepan with stock and season. Add the spiked onion and cook, stirring, over a medium heat until the cabbage softens. Discard the onion, bay leaf and garlic.

Place cabbage into greased gratin dish. Mix flour and curry powder with butter gradually adding cream until the mixture has a smooth consistency. Pour over cabbage and sprinkle with breadcrumbs. Bake at 180°C (350°F) for 15–20 minutes.

Serves 4

Note: Yoghurt may be substituted for cream. If so, you do not need to use any butter.

MUSHROOM MEDALLIONS

12 large mushroom caps
lemon juice
1 onion, finely chopped
4 bacon rashers
2 tablespoons melted butter

6 tablespoons breadcrumbs
1 tablespoon parsley
celery salt and black pepper

Prepare mushrooms by removing stalks and chopping them finely. Sprinkle inside the mushroom caps with lemon juice. Cook onion and chopped bacon in melted butter until the onion is soft. Add the breadcrumbs, parsley and seasonings. Fill the caps and heat through in the oven at 180°C (350°F).

Serves 6

CHINESE MUSHROOMS

12 large mushroom caps, wiped and trimmed if necessary

FILLING

250 g ground pork
1 tablespoon chopped shallots
1 egg
¼ cup minced water chestnuts
2 teaspoons grated fresh ginger

1 teaspoon soy sauce
fresh breadcrumbs (enough to combine ingredients into filling consistency)
sesame seeds

Combine all the ingredients, fill the prepared mushroom caps, sprinkle with sesame seeds and bake in 180°C (350°F) oven for 25 minutes.

Serves 6

POTATOES IN SHELLS

6 even-sized potatoes
1 tablespoon oil
1 celeriac root, peeled, cubed, boiled and drained
60 g butter
½ cup cream

2 egg yolks, reserve 1 egg white
salt and freshly ground pepper, to taste
4 tablespoons grated cheese

Scrub and dry the potatoes then rub with oil and bake, wrapped in foil, on a rack in the oven at 200°C (400°F) until tender.

Puree the cooked celeriac root and set aside, keeping warm. Cut a slice from the potatoes and scoop out potato leaving a firm shell. Mash the potato with butter and cream, add the celeriac, beat in the egg yolks and season to taste. Whisk the egg white and cut into the mixture. Fill the shells, top with grated cheese and bake at 200°C (400°F) until puffed and brown.

Serves 6

GRATIN DAUPHINOIS

750 g potatoes
salt and freshly ground black pepper
pinch nutmeg
1½ cups milk

½ cup cream
2 cloves crushed garlic
90 g grated Gruyere cheese
20 g butter

Wash and peel the potatoes then cut them into thin slices and arrange in layers in a greased gratin dish. Sprinkle top layer with salt and pepper and dust with nutmeg.

Combine the milk, cream and crushed garlic and pour over the potato layers. Sprinkle the top with grated Gruyere, dot with butter and cook in 200°C (400°F) oven for about 1 hour.

Serves 4–6

POMMES DE TERRE BOULANGERE

2 onions
750 g potatoes
60 g butter

1 cup stock, well-
 seasoned
ground black pepper

Slice the onions, blanch and drain them. Slice the potatoes thinly.

Grease gratin dish with 30 g butter and arrange the potatoes and onions alternately in layers, finishing with an overlapping layer of potatoes for the top. Season and dot with butter. Add the stock, pouring it in the side of the dish, then bake in 190°C (380°F) oven for about 1 hour, until brown.

Serves 4–6

EGGPLANT SHELLS

Shells: Slice unpeeled eggplants in half lengthways, salt lightly and stand 30 minutes to drain. Wipe dry and scoop out centre pulp. Use ½ shell for each person.

SAVOURY TOMATO FILLING

diced flesh of 6
 eggplants (aubergine)
 halves
1 garlic clove, crushed
2 onions, chopped

3 large tomatoes, peeled,
 seeded and chopped
2 tablespoons currants
3 tablespoons olive oil

TOPPING

½ cup oil
1 teaspoon sugar

salt and juice of 1 lemon
parsley to garnish

Simmer filling ingredients in olive oil until onion is soft, then pile into the prepared shells. Place in a baking dish and brush with oil combined with sugar and lemon juice. Fill dish with water halfway up shells, then cover and simmer gently until soft. Arrange on a serving dish and chill for 24 hours. Serve sprinkled with chopped parsley.

Serves 6

BRIOCHE FILLED WITH FRESH BEETROOT

8 medium-sized brioche
2–3 fresh beetroot,
 depending on size
juice of 1 orange
¾ cup mayonnaise

freshly ground black
 pepper
2 tablespoons chopped
 fresh dill
sprays of dill to garnish

Slice off the top ⅓ of the brioche and carefully remove most of the crumb. Break up the crumb and set aside.

Trim the beetroot stalks, leaving 2.5 cm, and wash. Cover the beetroot with cold water, bring to the boil, then reduce the heat and simmer, covered, until tender — about 20–40 minutes depending on the beetroot's size.

Drain beetroot and, wearing a pair of rubber gloves, slip the skins off. Trim the stalks and tail and dice when cool. Marinate in orange juice for 30 minutes, then drain.

Combine beetroot dice with the mayonnaise, using sufficient to bind the reserved brioche crumb. Add the pepper and dill. Chill until serving time. Just before serving, fill each brioche with the beetroot mixture, replace the 'lid' and garnish the plate with dill.

Serves 8

TOMATO SHELLS

500 g sliced green beans,
 crispy cooked then
 chilled

6 large tomatoes

DRESSING

2 tablespoons oil
1 tablespoon lemon juice
salt
finely chopped onion

1 tablespoon toasted
 sesame seeds
chopped seedless tomato
 pulp from shells

Prepare tomato shells by cutting the tomatoes in half and scooping out the pulp with a teaspoon. Reserve the pulp.

Combine dressing ingredients and toss with beans and tomato pulp. Fill tomato shells and serve, chilled, on lettuce leaves.

Serves 6

Brioche filled with Fresh Beetroot

PRAWN AND TOMATO SHELLS

8 even-sized ripe
    tomatoes
1 teaspoon gelatine
1 tablespoon water
½ cup mayonnaise
½ tablespoon lemon
    juice
dash of Angostura bitters

250 g medium-sized
    cooked prawns, shelled
    and deveined
1 tablespoon chopped dill
8 rounds of brown bread
    and butter sandwiches
watercress for garnishing

Skin the tomatoes, slice off the tops (reserve them), scoop out the seeds and drain the shells upside down.

Dissolve gelatine in water, add to the mayonnaise, season with lemon juice and bitters and leave to thicken slightly.

Coat prawns with dressing and sprinkle with the chopped dill. Fill shells and top with the caps.

Arrange each tomato on a sandwich round, garnished with watercress.

Serves 8

Broccoli and Celeriac Terrine

TOMATO AND CELERY CRESCENTS

1 tablespoon white wine
    vinegar
½ teaspoon dry mustard
salt and pepper, to taste

1 bunch celery heart
1 apple, diced
4 large tomato shells

DRESSING

3 tablespoons
    mayonnaise

3 tablespoons thick
    cream

Cut celery stalks, on an angle, into crescent-shaped slices, then chill them in an airtight container.

Mix together the dressing ingredients and toss with celery. Add the apple dice and fill the tomato cases. Top with chopped celery leaves and serve on crisp lettuce leaves.

Serves 4

BROCCOLI AND CELERIAC TERRINE

600 g broccoli florets,
    stalks trimmed
4 egg whites, used 2 at a
    time
salt and white pepper
⅛ teaspoon nutmeg and
    ground ginger

⅓–½ cup thickened
    (double) cream, lightly
    whipped
450 g celeriac, peeled
garlic salt
butter for greasing
aspic jelly (savoury)

MAYONNAISE COLLEE

2 tablespoons white wine
1 tablespoon white
    vinegar

2 tablespoons clear stock
1 tablespoon gelatine
1½ cups mayonnaise

Cook the broccoli florets in boiling salted water until tender. Refresh in cold water and drain thoroughly. Set aside 150 g of the florets for garnishing and puree the rest. Beat 2 egg whites, a little at a time, into the puree, then add seasonings and flavourings. Stand over ice and beat in the cream, a little at a time.

Quarter the celeriac and cook in boiling salted water until soft. Puree, beat in 2 egg whites and season as with the broccoli.

Grease a terrine with butter, and layer alternately with broccoli and celeriac fillings. Cover with greased greaseproof paper and the lid and cook for 45 minutes in a water bath until set. Water should only simmer.

Pour wine, vinegar and stock into a bowl and add gelatine to soften. Stand in hot water to dissolve then cool until tepid. Beat gradually into the mayonnaise and season if necessary.

When the terrine is cool, top with the Mayonnaise Collee and remaining broccoli florets, then spoon over the light aspic.

Serves 4

CRAB-STUFFED CUCUMBER

2 large cucumbers
1 can crabmeat

squeeze lemon juice
dash Tabasco

EGG AND VINEGAR DRESSING

2 egg yolks
1 tablespoon stock
1 tablespoon sugar

3 tablespoons vinegar
salt

Lightly peel cucumber and remove centre. Flake crabmeat, add the flavourings, fill the cucumber shells and chill, covered.

Combine egg yolks, stock, sugar, vinegar and salt in china bowl and whisk over hot water until thickened. When cool, slice the filled cucumber shells into thick rings, 2 on each plate, and serve with 1 tablespoon of dressing on the side.

Serves 6

AVOCADO MOUSSE

20 g gelatine, soaked in
  ⅓ cup cold water
⅓ cup chicken stock,
  boiling
1¾ cup avocado pulp
1 teaspoon onion juice

2 teaspoons
  Worcestershire sauce
½ cup mayonnaise
½ cup cream, lightly
  whipped

SALAD

2 small green capsicums
  (peppers)
black olives

2 tablespoons Vinaigrette
  Dressing (see recipe)
red pimiento threads

Oil a 5-cup ring mould. Dissolve the soaked gelatine in boiling stock and add to the avocado pulp with onion juice and Worcestershire sauce. When cold, fold in the mayonnaise and lightly whipped cream. Pour into prepared mould, cover and leave to set in the refrigerator.

Shred the capsicum, blanch in boiling water, drain and refresh. Halve and stone the olives combine with capsicum and toss with Vinaigrette Dressing. Add the pimiento threads.

Unmould to serve, filling the centre with the salad vegetables.

Serves 4–6

CURRIED POTATO SALAD

6 large potatoes,
  scrubbed
½ cup French Dressing
  (see recipe)
1 onion, chopped
1 cup sliced celery
1 small green capsicum
  (pepper), seeded and
  chopped

2 cups mayonnaise
1 tablespoon curry
  powder
salt and pepper
8 lettuce cups
green capsicum (pepper),
  for garnish

Cook potatoes until just tender. Cool slightly, peel, slice, place in a bowl and pour over French Dressing. Cover and chill.

Blend ¼ cup mayonnaise with curry powder, salt and pepper and then combine with the remaining mayonnaise. Mix the potatoes, onions and celery and fold in the mayonnaise. Arrange in lettuce cups, garnished with chopped green pepper.

Pumpkin may be substituted for potatoes and caraway seeds added for a different flavouring.

Serves 8

PRAWN AND PAWPAW SALAD

1 pawpaw, about 1 kg
1 lemon
1 orange
¾ cup mayonnaise
¼ cup cream
2 tablespoons chopped
  dill

750 g medium-sized
  cooked prawns, shelled
  and deveined
freshly ground black
  pepper
fresh dill sprigs, to
  garnish

Halve the pawpaw, scoop out the seeds, peel and cut into slices, lengthways. Carefully peel the rind only of the lemon and orange. Cut into julienne strips, blanch in boiling water for 5 minutes, drain, refresh and reserve for garnishing. Squeeze the juice of both fruits.

Prawn and Pawpaw Salad

Combine the mayonnaise with lemon and orange juice to taste. Whip the cream until thickened and soft peaks form then gently fold into the mayonnaise with the dill.

Arrange the pawpaw slices and prawns on a serving plate, sprinkle with freshly ground pepper then spoon over the mayonnaise. Garnish with fresh dill sprigs and the orange and lemon rind.

Serves 6

VEGETABLE SALAD

2 cups cauliflower florets
1 cup each chopped red
    capsicum (pepper) and
    green capsicum

1 cup sliced button
    mushrooms
½ cup almond slivers,
    toasted

DRESSING

1 tablespoon white wine
    vinegar
½ tablespoon tarragon

salt and pepper to taste
⅓ cup vegetable oil

Parboil the cauliflower and capsicum, drain then refresh them. Chill for 2 hours in a bowl covered with the combined dressing ingredients. Add the mushroom slices, toss and stand the salad at room temperature for 1 hour. Check seasoning and serve sprinkled with the almonds.

Serves 4

FRENCH DRESSING

French Dressing is a must with green salad vegetables, tomatoes and cucumber.

¼ cup white wine
   vinegar
salt
freshly ground black
   pepper
½ teaspoon sugar

½ teaspoon mustard
   powder
1 clove garlic, peeled and
   lightly pressed
½ cup olive oil

Combine vinegar, salt and pepper, sugar, mustard and garlic in a screw-topped jar or blender. Shake or process until well-blended. Gradually add the oil and mix until combined.

Makes ¾ cup

VINAIGRETTE

½ cup white wine
   vinegar
salt and freshly ground
   black pepper
1 cup oil

Shake or process all ingredients in a screw-topped jar or blender until well combined.

Makes 1½ cups

GLOSSARY OF COOKING TERMS

Baste Spoon or pour liquid or fat over food as it cooks to prevent drying out or loss of flavour.

Blanch To pre-cook very briefly — usually vegetables.

Blend Combining two or more ingredients so they are completely mixed together and inseparable. Can be done by hand or in blender or food processor.

Cream To stir or beat an ingredient until it is smooth and lump-free.

Cut In With clean strokes of knife or spatula mix, say, fat or egg whites into other ingredients without softening or flattening them in the process.

Dice Cut into small squares.

Flame Set alight with alcohol while cooking.

Fold Blend in gently without losing air from, say, whipped ingredients.

Fricassee Browning to seal while covered in a little flour, then simmering gently to tenderise.

Glaze Film surface of tart or piece of meat with sugar syrup or clear coating.

Knead Handling dough to make it smooth and elastic — folding one half on top of the other, then pressing together, turning and repeating process.

Puree Mixing together or blending ingredients to make soft, lump-free paste.

Refresh Dip or rinse already cooked food — usually vegetables — in cold water.

Saute Brown over high heat until outside is crisp but inside is lightly cooked and tender.

Season Add flavour with herbs, spices, salt or pepper.

Sweat Cook gently over flame so that ingredients soften but do not brown.

Index

Printed in Singapore